ABOVE, ALONG, INSIDE, AND THROUGH

Poems, Prayers, and Reflections

Dear Cetta —
Thank you for
sharing this
wonderful afternoon!
Peace and Blessings,
Lisa Wagner
Carbllo

ABOVE,

ALONG,

INSIDE,

AND

THROUGH

Poems, Prayers, and Reflections

LISA WAGNER-CAROLLO

Photography by
CHRIS CAROLLO

Ayasofya
PRESS

Above, Along, Inside, and Through
Poems, Prayers, and Reflections
Copyright © Lisa Wagner-Carollo 2017, Reprinted 2020

Foreword: Jim Forest
Photography: Chris Carollo
Editors: Annalise Raziq and Adept Content Solutions
Interview: Mary A. DuQuaine
Cover and Book Design: Nelson Kane

Some names and identifying details have been changed to protect the privacy of individuals.

For permission requests, contact publisher via website below:

Ayasofya Press
Chicago, IL
www.aya.press

Library of Congress Control Number: 2017957387
ISBN-10: 1-944510-04-4 ISBN-13: 978-1-944510-04-6
ebook
ISBN-10: 1-944510-05-2 ISBN-13: 978-1-944510-05-3

First Edition

Printed in the United States of America

This book is dedicated to my parents, Richard and Shirley Wagner

and

to my husband, Chris Carollo

Contents

⟶✹ Foreword

I live near Amsterdam; Lisa Wagner in Chicago. Though our homes are seven time zones apart, I regard Lisa as one of my neighbors. We're two of the many people living elbow-to-elbow in the spacious, one-time-zone household of Dorothy Day.

We got to meet for the first time when she recruited me (this in the days of paper letters and lick-on-the-back postage stamps) to help set up a performance in Amsterdam of her Dorothy Day play. The local Catholic Worker community was the real organizer. All I had to do was connect a few dots, make a few phone calls, design a poster, and offer Lisa use of our guest bed. The University of Amsterdam gave us performance space, and by some miracle every chair was filled. It was standing room only.

Lisa's one-woman performance was astonishing. A young actress became a convincing, compelling, challenging Dorothy Day both for me, who had lived and worked with Dorothy, but, far more important, for a crowd of people who knew next to nothing about Dorothy Day. There was a standing ovation at the end.

Lisa is both a storyteller and a story liver. Through her theatrical art, she has told and retold the stories of Dorothy Day and other brave women whose lives bear witness to the Gospel and has done so without sprinkling confectioner's sugar on any of her heroes. Between performances she has lived the story in her own unique Lisa Wagner way. Her art is deeply rooted in her offstage life.

In this collection of journal entries and poetry, Lisa lifts the curtain on her more-hidden life, with the joys and agonies of community life in houses of hospitality one of her principal themes. One of Lisa's discoveries in pursuing such a demanding, interruption-packed life has been the necessity of occasionally taking a U-turn toward solitude—"wasting time with God," as she puts it in these pages.

One of the major threads running through these pages is Lisa's two-decade struggle to come to terms with the suicide of her brother Mark. As her account bears witness, grieving often begins with prolonged numbness until at some point the dike breaks and explodes into anger—"How could you do this to me? How could you wound me so deeply?" Lisa describes a complex journey that brought her from almost paralyzing rage to deep, tear-soaked grieving and finally to profound forgiveness.

One of the simple truths Lisa reminds me of is how much stories matter—in fact, how life defining stories are. Sadly, for many people their mainspring story is about good people having to kill bad people—the hero as killer. The courageous women Lisa brings to life onstage—the same women who inspire her offstage life—kill no one.

Lisa reminds me the extent to which one's life is shaped by exemplars. It becomes easier to live an adventurous life, a life in which love becomes a more powerful force than fear, when you discover others who model vocations that had once seemed totally out of reach. Loving others, loving enemies, and loving God is not just for the few who seem born to walk on the high wires of God's circus. "We're all called to be saints," as Dorothy Day said so often.

Jim Forest, 4 July 2016

Acknowledgements

First of all, I wish to acknowledge Mary DuQuaine, Danielle Chapman, Annalise Raziq, and Margaret McClory for their support and encouragement in the process of creating this work.

As I reflect on the unfolding of this book, I realize that many people have walked with me. Among these individuals are the healers in my life who have offered deep listening and compassion: Anne Luther, Randi Kant, Rita Tresnowski, and Jessica Hazel. I am also grateful for the Ravenswood Presbyterian Youth Group. They have uplifted my spirit on many Friday evenings. I would also like to extend thanks to the community of Still Point Theatre Collective— to all the artists who have worked diligently throughout the years with compassion and dedication. Anita Dacanay has long been part of the Still Point community, and I am deeply grateful to her for twenty-five years of nurturing friendship.

I also wish to thank my family—my siblings, Shari and David, and their spouses and children. And finally, I offer gratitude to my parents, Richard and Shirley Wagner, and to my husband, Chris Carollo.

ABOVE, ALONG, INSIDE, AND THROUGH

I trace my finger along the mountain ridge.
The trees gently bend beneath my touch.
My hands smooth the tops of the mountains,
and tickle the laughing waters.

I part the foliage and find myself—

hidden
under green leaves.

So small, shaking,
in awe of the vastness.

Still, I move—
above, along, inside—and through—the mystery of creation,
and myself.

The balding youth leader invited me to sit in the shotgun seat of the white van. We were on our way to Jellystone Park—of Yogi Bear fame—in Branson, Missouri. My friend Leigh had invited me on the trip with her youth group from Colonial Presbyterian Church: the stately, gigantic, white-pillared church at the corner of 95th and Wornall. I settled into the seat and slammed the car door. I put on my seatbelt, and our group pulled out of the Shell station.

I smiled at the balding youth leader. I was only fifteen, but I knew why I was sitting in this beige front seat, the vinyl sticking to my tanned thighs. This was "get to know you time." You see, I was the new girl. I was not a frequent youth group attendee.

He was a kind man. He wore a gold cross around his neck that dangled from a gold chain. He was also sincere and had a peacefulness, a "smug peace" about him. We talked about school. I don't think I told him I had been named "Outstanding Girl Citizen" of my ninth-grade class because that probably would've felt like bragging to my modest, fifteen-year-old psyche. However, I did tell him that I loved theater.

I stared ahead, smiling softly and politely, as he worked hard to keep the van at exactly fifty-five miles per hour. Finally, after the small talk diminished, he asked me: "Are you a Christian?"

This group was more evangelical than the Lutherans I grew up with. I shrugged my shoulders. "Ya know, I've really been a Christian all my life. I really don't understand when people talk about 'becoming a Christian.' I've just always been one."

He tilted his head slightly. I could tell he was carefully weighing his response.

"Well, you know, it's really more than that—it's a day to day commitment—it's about committing your entire life to Christ."

I squinted my eyes at him as the billboards skipped past us.

"I don't know—I just know that I've always been one."

He smiled politely, making eye contact briefly, and then returned his eyes to the road.

We arrived at Jellystone. An enormous billboard splashed with the likenesses of Yogi Bear and Boo-Boo met us at the park entrance. We settled in, and there were campfires, Bibles, and a lot of talk about Jesus.

One evening, sitting around the campfire, I thought of my home church, Bethany Lutheran, back home. I thought of Pastor Sabo flinging his arms from the pulpit—with his enormous enthusiasm. I was recently confirmed at Bethany. I went through confirmation classes in the groovy-painted youth group room. I remembered the psychedelic, purple butterflies on the youth group walls. I remembered memorizing scripture passages and sections of the Lutheran Catechism.

During my classes, I had felt overwhelmed by all of the memorization, and it all seemed like only an "exercise" to me, beyond my comprehension. But I also experienced, in short flashes, a longing, a deep sense of being drawn to something beyond myself.

The youth group room was on the first floor. I would sit on one of the brown couches, leftover from the 1960s, and gaze at the mural-like paintings from the 1970s (dripping from the cinder block walls). Three of the boys in my class were restless, and they flew around the room like pasta being chased across a plate, throwing pencils and chalk at each other's wiry, hormonally confused frames. The forty-something director of religious education seemed completely at a loss when it came to controlling these three boys. At the end of class one day, the boys darted out of the room, and the bespectacled teacher did not move. He remained in his chair, his eyes to the ground, and his shoulders hunched. He shook his head with the heaviness of defeat and disillusionment. I sat still on the couch, sadness and compassion for this man overtaking my fear of scripture memorization.

Finally, the day of confirmation arrived. We filed into the church wearing white robes and red carnations. The pipe organ loomed behind us. I "feathered" my hair in those days—and it would take at least an hour to achieve this important "feathered" look. However, even after an hour of work, my thin, lifeless hair would require several layers of VO5 Hairspray to maintain the "feathered" effect for hours to come. With all of these sprayed layers, my hair was no longer a series of separate strands but had morphed into one solid structure—such that if a strong wind blew from the north, the entire entity would rise as one single, rock-like form. Also, the multilayer spray requirement removed the shine from my locks. My mane no longer "shone," but "reflected," the surface now being comparable to the shellac on a kiln-fired plate of pottery.

So, I processed into the church, white robed and reflecting. The confirmation candidates sat in the first few rows, looking straight ahead to the floor-to-ceiling glass windows behind the altar and the tall wooden cross planted in the ground outside.

The service began and unfolded in the usual fashion. I was nervous. I shifted in my seat and fingered my bulletin with ten sweaty digits.

At last, the time for our confirmation ceremony arrived. Pastor Sabo walked toward us, gesturing wildly. I rubbed my hands together as he began to call each of us forward, one by one. Each candidate, when it was their time, kneeled in front of Pastor Sabo. He would place a hand on their head, say a prayer, and announce:

"And your scripture verse is . . ." I shifted harder in the pew.

Scripture verse? What scripture verse? An outstanding girl citizen has usually done her due diligence. I panicked. I asked myself, "Were we supposed to choose a scripture verse?"

Doom and disaster surrounded me as I realized that I had not chosen a scripture verse.

The candidates continued to file forward. We were processing to the fore in alphabetical order, and since my last name was "Wagner" I had plenty of time to agonize.

"Oh no! A scripture verse!" The panic rose.

I had visions of kneeling before Pastor Sabo and his leaning his square face next to mine and whispering with annoyance, "You didn't submit a scripture verse! What is your verse?!"

It was clear, I needed to think of a verse. I tried. Even though I'd spent months memorizing scripture—all for this day, my mind blanked. They were already to the S's in the line, and there were only three candidates ahead of me. Suddenly, the words "The Lord is my shepherd, I shall not want" sprang to my fevered mind.

"That's it!" I thought, "If he asks me what my scripture verse is, I'll tell him that one! That's it!"

Charlie Upton, brown-haired and freckled, kneeled in front of Pastor Sabo. His confirming ritual was completed in what seemed like an instant. I walked one-two-three-four-five steps to the kneeler. I slowly kneeled and bowed my head. Pastor Sabo recited a prayer. I waited for a moment, waited for him to lean forward to ask me what verse I had chosen, which I had so incompetently failed to submit. However, he didn't lean forward. Instead, he placed a wide, square hand on my head and said, "And your scripture verse, Lisa, is 'The Lord is my shepherd, I shall not want.'"

I opened my closed eyes, full of surprise. I stood up, and he smiled at me. I walked back to the pew slowly, a soft smile of wonder growing on my lips.

This memory washed over me as I sat by the bonfire in Branson, gazing into the orange-yellow flames. I thought about the verse, and once again the wonder I felt that day washed over me.

The next day, our last day at Jellystone, I took my Bible and went to find a quiet place. I found a toppled log lying under a tree on the side of a lake. I sat on the log and looked out at the water. I felt serenity and gratitude. I thought about the longing I had felt in confirmation class. I thought of the Sunday services at Bethany Lutheran Church. I thought of the sincere youth leader with the smug peace. I had told him that I was a Christian—and I was. I picked at the log and threw a piece of bark into the water.

But he was saying, over the last couple of days, that God and Jesus could be a part of every single day of our lives. Even though I was a Christian already, this fact was new to me. At my feet, I saw the shadows of leaves move across a stone, and once again,

I felt the longing inside of me. I looked across the lake. A bird fluttered in the branches above me. I said a prayer: "God, Jesus, if you can be part of every day of my life, please, I want to do that."

That afternoon, our group of youth left the park, heading home to Kansas City, and Yogi Bear and Boo-Boo, wide-eyed and smiling, watched us as our white van drove away.

—⚜ Preface

March, 1992. I sat on the edge of a narrow twin bed in a tiny room. The window was open only slightly, and a soft breeze lifted a blue curtain. My feet rested on the brown-and-beige tile floor, my hands on my knees. I looked at the swirl of brown and beige on the tiles. I breathed in the serenity in the air. I looked up at the white wall and down at the red, blue, green, and yellow patchwork quilt on the bed. I heard a dog bark a block or two away. I heard voices in the hall. This brick building, on the west side of Chicago, had formerly been inhabited by a group of young and eager Catholic sisters who packed this building in the 1950s. But now, it was inhabited by a group of young volunteers who assisted the few remaining Sinsinawa Dominican sisters in their work. They called themselves the Connections Community. My dear friend, Lisa Simone, lived in this house.

A week before, I had wept as I told Lisa of my exhaustion and how I felt besieged by my countless commitments. We sat in a café, and I rattled off my litany of responsibilities: living full time at St. Catherine's Catholic Worker with formerly homeless men and women living with AIDS, touring the country with my one-woman show on Dorothy Day, teaching a theater class to adults with developmental disabilities at Esperanza Community Services, and working fifteen hours a week at Tobias House, a group home of Esperanza. Lisa looked at me with her dark Sicilian eyes and listened, grounded and compassionate. As the words swirled between us, we discerned that I needed to temporarily eliminate at least one of my commitments so that I could regain my grounding and regain strength. She immediately suggested that I come to stay with her community for a couple of weeks, temporarily moving out of the Catholic Worker house. As I reached into my bulging purse for a wadded, already-used Kleenex, I silently nodded in agreement. She said she would check with her housemates to make sure there was a room available and let me know as soon as possible.

Now, seven days had passed, and I sat on the narrow bed. The room was almost silent.

The air was still and serene. I breathed another deep, full breath, and let this new, almost foreign peacefulness sink into my belly. The infinite to-do list that continuously haunted me seemed to recede and disappear into a corner of this tiny room. As the army of demands seemed to retreat, I began to realize how tired I was. I was a husk. I was dried up, brittle, and empty. I was completely charred.

I stared at the floor and wondered how I had come to this place. For many years, I had felt a deep call to serve. Thirteen years before, as a fifteen-year-old, sitting on the edge of a lake in the middle of the Ozarks, I had fallen in love with the Divine Spirit and had felt led to leave all behind to love. And now, this grand call had gotten me here—listening to a dog in the distance and sensing the gargantuan shakiness of my spirit. I had given and given, feeling that this giving of myself was my call. But, if I was called, why was I now so lost, shaken, and empty? I lay down on the bed, still relishing the peace but also aware that I needed to set a course for healing.

Two weeks later, I returned to the Catholic Worker House and continued my discernment. One quiet evening, I sat at our lumbering, oak dining room table and shared with one of the other Catholic workers my new awareness and need for healing. Unexpectedly, I began to speak of the Tacoma L'Arche community in Tacoma, Washington, where I had experienced many joyful days visiting fellow L'Arche assistants. I had been an assistant for two years at L'Arche Heartland in Kansas City, sharing my life with adults with developmental disabilities, and I had often gone to Tacoma for vacations and retreats. As I spoke of the Tacoma community, a light ignited inside of me. I suddenly knew that if I returned to Tacoma and committed myself to an extended retreat, I could begin to heal.

Early October, 1992, I arrived at L'Arche Tacoma's prayer house, Hope Spring, for a forty-nine-day retreat. Often, people have earnestly asked, "why forty-nine days?" The answer is simple: two months before my Tacoma sojourn, I had disentangled myself from all of my Chicago commitments, moved back into my parents' house to earn money for the retreat, and had given a month and a half of my life to Crum and Forster

Commercial Insurance as a temp. Through my daily collating and copying, I had saved $490. The retreat center charged ten dollars a day. Consequently, I had just enough cash for a forty-nine-day retreat.

I spent my forty-nine days taking long walks in the insistent, almost daily rain, journaling, meeting with my spiritual director, praying in the center's chapel, and simply wasting time with God. I didn't have any post-retreat plans, so the first two weeks were spent fighting off anxiety and thoughts that screamed, *What have I done? What am I going to do after this?* After finally making friends with this unease, I began to let go and to see my life in sharp relief. One night, I sat and gazed at the stars and realized that without all of the duties that I had let define me, all I had left was the Divine—and myself. I scrawled a poem in my spiral notebook called "Me, God, and Stars." Deep in my core, I began to consider the idea that this essential "beingness" might be enough.

After my Tacoma retreat came to a close, I took a Greyhound bus to the Nestucca Sanctuary, a retreat center on the coast of Oregon. Two weeks before, a priest friend in Tacoma, Fr. Bill Bichsel, had placed an envelope holding $35 for bus fare into my hand. He radiantly smiled and said, "You just gotta see it."

Nestucca was a Jesuit-run center situated on a peninsula and also served as a wildlife sanctuary. At Nestucca, I encountered dew-drenched ferns, towering fir trees, creeping moss, and gentle fawns and does, quietly bent over, chewing grass. All of the insights, quiet revelations, and epiphanies I had experienced on my Tacoma retreat sank even more deeply into my spirit.

One bright afternoon, I stood on the farthest edge of the peninsula. The green abundance laughed all around me, surrounding me like a wave of bursting life. Below, a clear river wound its way to the ocean, and, only a few hundred feet away, in the distance, the wild sea crashed against towering black rocks.

I stood there, and remembered the brown and beige tile floor. I remembered my dried-out, exhausted soul, and the narrow twin bed. I remembered myself, trying too hard to please and accomplish. The waves crashed against the rocks in the distance, and I realized that I was no longer dried out and hollow, but that once again life and fecundity surged through my being. I realized that all of this harsh expectation that I had swallowed whole and internalized—this expectation to please—and to "get things done"—to prove myself—all of it was a lie.

Life—true, full, abundant, crazy life was mine—no matter what I did or didn't achieve.

Over these last forty-some days, through walks in the rain and quiet nights in the candlelit chapel, I had looked through the glass of my life. I had seen the tangled knots of fear and unhealthy drive, but I had also seen the gift of the Divine and the utterly amazing mystery of my own existence. As I stood there, surrounded by so much splendor, I felt as if my initial epiphany, sitting under the stars in Tacoma, had wonderfully ripened and fully taken root.

It's been more of a journey from that revelatory moment on the peninsula in Oregon to the birth of this book. My experience there brought into sharp relief the tension I have often felt between my undeniable awareness of our Divine Genesis and the sometimes agonizing "push and pull" of everyday life. After I returned to Chicago, I continued to sometimes float—but often, stagger—through my daily experiences. I continued to move above, along, inside, and through traffic jams, irritable store clerks, loyal friends, peaceful evenings, stubbed toes, cherubim children on the train, long, soothing embraces, and sleepless nights. And, through these doors and turned corners, I believe the Divine was there—and is here—holding and guiding me as I move through each day, even during the times that I have felt utterly alone and spiritually orphaned. This book is simply the murmurings that have emerged from this daily living. Some of the words were written on a bus, some on retreat, and others were expelled at the end of a long, frustrating day. I could've kept them in a cardboard box in my closet (where many of them have been—tucked away in spiral notebooks), but, over time, I've developed a sense that others could benefit from reading these words—at least this is my prayer.

Maybe you will find some comfort in these words, at the end of your own long day, or perhaps you can open to a page while sitting in an airport when your flight has been delayed, and the fingers of frustration begin to scratch. Or, maybe you can open to a particularly relevant poem while sitting on the edge of your own peninsula, away and alone.

I encourage you to use this book in a way that is meaningful and helpful to you. It is divided into four sections. The first section, *Above*, meditates on the elusiveness and closeness of Divine Mystery. The *Along* segment explores relationships with others and all of creation, and *Inside* searches and probes the inner journey. The final section, *Through*, examines the quest for healing as we move through life experiences that are deeply painful—experiences that we doubt we will ever survive.

As I've inferred, you don't necessarily need to read this book straight through, but you may simply open to a poem, prayer, or reflection that you find particularly relevant to your current life experience, as joyous or tangled as it may be. If reading is not what you desire, simply let your eyes fall upon one of Chris Carollo's photographs, and allow the image to brush over you or sink deep within.

The murmurings and images on these pages are now yours to hold as you move above, along, inside, and through the mystery and surprise of your own unique journey.

ABOVE

There have been moments when I've awakened at dawn, and in the stillness of the morning, I've sensed a deep mysterious force dwelling in my spirit. I sense that this Divine force had no genesis in a way I cannot comprehend. It has simply always been.

At these moments, I'm overwhelmed with gratitude that I'm a part of creation and, at the same time, overwhelmed with a realization that I'll never fully understand it all. This understanding is above my reach. However, even with this realization, I still sense the closeness of God. When I was twenty-eight years old, I met a man named Joe Douglass, who created a space in my life, an opening to the mysteries of the Divine.

Joe's eyes were wide—big brown eyes. He sat in the red-carpeted foyer of St. Catherine's Catholic Worker, thin and weak, his light brown skin growing paler. He wore a t-shirt that read, "Love Life—Stop AIDS." St. Catherine's was a house of hospitality on the south side of Chicago for men and women who were homeless and living with HIV or AIDS. Twenty of us lived together in a former rectory, twelve guests and eight Catholic workers. We lived as an intentional community, the workers running the house, answering the door, taking shifts in the office, cooking meals, and gathering for morning and evening prayer. The workers received room, board, and sixty dollars a month for spending money.

I lived at St. Catherine's from 1990 until 1992, and it was in early May of 1991 that Joe sat in the foyer. He had just returned from Cook County Hospital and was living through his end stages. A rumor was flying around the house that he did not want to return to the hospital but instead wanted to stay at St. Catherine's and receive hospice care from the community. Through evening meals in the dining room, casual conversations "hanging around" the office door, and rides to and from the hospital, the community had become his family. He wished to die among us. After verifying the rumor as fact, we had a staff meeting, and decided to extend hospice care to Joe. We set up a room for him next to the kitchen, and began caring for him.

Spring was turning to summer, and Joe's room became a frequent haunt for workers and guests alike. Joe and I would sit together in his narrow room with the window open. It was a familiar space, having been our chapel before we moved the prayer books, candles and incense to a room in the front of the house. Joe's new space had white walls and dark brown wood-work, twelve-foot ceilings, and a window facing west. Joe and I would sit together, speaking very little, simply watching TV, Joe wrapped in a soft blue blanket.

One sweltering afternoon, we were watching a soap opera, and a couple toppled into each other's arms. Joe glanced over at me, "If everyone just made love," he noted, "the world would be a better place." Another day, I stopped by Joe's room on my way to buy a new pair of sandals. I told him of my mission, and departed for Payless Shoe Source. A few hours later, I returned home, and found my way up to my room on the second floor. I was just settling in when one of the other workers knocked on my door and said, "Joe wants to see your new shoes." I ran down to Joe's room to show him my sandals. He sat up, swung his legs over the side of the bed, looked at my shoes, and said, "Nice."

Joe and I were becoming friends, and I felt privileged that I had been invited to spend the last days of his life with him. However, I also sensed myself becoming agitated and depressed. One afternoon, I was driving down Lake Shore Drive, trying desperately to get to an important meeting on time. I grumbled at myself for leaving the house late. I found the road blocked by a stalled bus. I pounded the steering wheel and screamed an obscenity. I felt the anger begin in my stomach, spread up through my chest, down through my legs, and out to my fingertips and toes. I finally arrived at the meeting. I tried to listen and participate, though the anger still smoldered like a hot coal in my stomach.

Afterwards, I gave my friend, Paul, a ride home. The traffic stopped. Cars cut in front of us. The menacing orange barrels and cones appeared everywhere. I gripped the steering wheel and told my friend of my distress.

"You really need therapy," he quipped. "You have anger coming out everywhere."

I complained about the city. We pulled onto I-290. I griped about work. We exited at Austin Avenue. Suddenly, I began to talk about my brother, Mark, who had committed suicide ten years before. My words surprised me. I thought I had worked through so much of my grief, and now, suddenly, the grief surged back, intense and intrusive. We arrived at Paul's apartment. He got out of the car.

"Why are you always around when I'm having a breakdown?" I asked.

"I guess you trust me," he said, and then added jokingly, "Lucky me."

I pulled back onto I-290. I thought about my brother. I began crying as I moved past the cars. The violence of his death seemed to be pulling me under. I cried and said over and over, "He shot himself in the head. He shot himself in the head."

The next day, I sat in our brown paneled community room with the other eight Catholic workers, my "community mates." The wind gently lifted the white chiffon curtains as I told them about my quiet afternoons with Joe, the new sandals, the sweetness of his interest and care, and how grateful I felt to be spending the last days of his life with him. I also told them about my agitation on Lake Shore Drive, the banging of the steering wheel, and my hot tears as I barreled along I-290—the thoughts of my brother erupting unexpectedly. As the others listened, it became obvious what was happening to me: being in the same house with Joe was stirring parts of me that had not yet grieved for my brother. He was about the same age that my brother would've been if he had lived, and he was struggling with drug addiction, as my brother had. The community assured me that I needed to be gentle with myself. We agreed that since it felt like my brother's death had just happened, I needed to hold myself gently, as if it had truly just happened. I needed time away.

I took my time away with the School Sisters of Notre Dame in their convent on Pine Avenue. For a week and a half, I was able to rest in my Lilliputian tiled room and reflect in the sisters' white carpeted chapel. I meditated on my peaceful afternoons with Joe, attempted to air the fragments of my psyche that still ached for my brother, and listened for God's murmurings. I was grateful to have space, but I missed my community mates, the music and prayer in the chapel, and the endless conversations around the dining room table. I visited St. Catherine's often.

After I had been gone for ten days, I stopped by the house for a birthday party the guests were throwing for our live-in volunteer, Michael. They had decorated the dining room with white balloons and streamers. Hot food steamed on the table: chicken and vegetables that glistened with butter. It was a true celebration. Four guests read birthday cards out loud to Michael. We sang "Happy Birthday" and, at one point, even did the wave around the dining room table. The time flew by.

Relaxed and happy, I was about to head out, when one of the workers, Al, appeared in the entrance of the dining room. He leaned wearily against the doorway, and reported that Joe was not doing well.

A few of us darted into Joe's room. We found him breathing heavily. He threw all of his strength and energy into each gasp for air. We quietly stood around him. Al took his hand, Tom wiped his forehead, and Katia, who was an RN, offered him a water-soaked sponge on a tiny plastic stick, for Joe's lips were scorched. We stood together, held fast by each strained breath. He could barely talk, of course, but when Katia sneezed, he said, as clear as day, "God bless you." We laughed, as the tension splintered between us like thin ice on a river. Katia leaned against my shoulder, sighed, and called for a meeting in the office. Tom remained with Joe, while the rest of us gathered quietly down the hall, leaning against the old school desk and the filing cabinet. We listened, as Katia ascertained that Joe probably wouldn't live through the weekend.

My body felt slow and heavy as I left the house. The plans I had made earlier in the day were calling me, and yet, for obvious reasons, my spirit was not eager to leave Joe's side.

I slid into my brown Nova and drove to pick up my friend, Kathy. We made our way to the west side of town where our friend was having a summer solstice party, but Joe might as well have been with us. His presence was palpable.

We reached the party, and gathered on the rooftop for an uplifting celebration. I stood with others in a circle around a small bonfire, the yellowed city lights flickering on all sides. I looked at the faces of my friends in the circle and strained to focus, but my mind was back at St. Catherine's, hovering in a corner of Joe's room. At 12:30, I pulled Kathy aside and told her that I needed to go home. I was afraid that Joe had already died.

We drove back to the south side. I dropped off Kathy and began the five-minute journey to St. Catherine's.

"Please let him still be alive," I prayed, as I waited for red lights to change and cars to turn.

At last, I pulled up in front of the house. I looked in the rectangular office window and noticed that three workers were standing around, conversing in a relaxed fashion. I knew from their body language that Joe was still alive. Relieved, I walked into the house and gathered with the others in the office. Katia had just spoken on the phone with the hospice nurse and had begun to prepare a prescribed medication for Joe.

"I think I'll go see him," I told my friends, and made my way to Joe's room.

Isaac, one of our guests, was sitting with Joe when I walked through the door. "Can you sit with him awhile?" he asked, "I need a smoke break."

He left, and I sat in a chair next to Joe's bed. His demeanor had changed. He was no longer breathing heavily. He was taking small breaths and wasn't as aware as he had been before. His eyes were looking away from me at the northern, white wall. I had only sat with him for a few minutes when Katia entered with the medicine she had prepared. She looked at Joe. Her face fell.

"Oh," her voice trailed off. She put the medicine down. "I don't think you'll be needing this anymore." She stood next to him, touching his face and arm, and speaking quietly. "Thank you, Joe. Thank you for the past few months. We love you."

I don't know how much time passed, but some moments later, Joe's body relaxed, and his face turned towards us. He had died.

It is hard to describe what I experienced at that moment. It was as if a door opened, just slightly, and I saw beyond our surface reality and saw more than we could ever imagine . . . more love, more depth, more beauty, more than is comprehensible. It was as if the hidden ground of being, the vast Divine Mystery, had opened for a brief moment. I felt as if Joe's life had left him and spilled onto us. Since I had not been with my brother at the moment of his death, being with Joe at the time of his crossing was incredibly healing for me. Witnessing and experiencing, if only for an instant, the hidden ground of being in Joe's passage assured me that my brother also dwelt peacefully—somewhere—on that holy ground.

One month later, on my brother's birthday, July 22, I sat in the community chapel with my fellow Catholic workers and several friends. With psalms and silence, we celebrated a special Mass of the Resurrection for Mark Alan Wagner. Katia had suggested we celebrate this ritual as a way to mark my experience of reawakened grief and healing. Between the readings and prayers, I reflected on the healing I had experienced through Joe's death. Unknowingly, he had reunited my fractured spirit with the spirit of my brother.

Katia and my friend Paul, who had been in the car with me during my initial breaking, played their guitars. I had a photograph of my brother, sporting a thick, brown bowtie, displayed on the altar. I had selected special readings, and one of them was the story of the resurrection of Lazarus. I felt myself saying with Martha in Bethany, "Lord, if you would've been here, my brother would not have died." But I also felt with her the awe and wonder of the resurrection, which had fallen open before me, even in the midst of doubt and pain.

Holy One, grant us the grace to celebrate the mystery of every step, to live in wonder and gratitude for all that is above our reach.

CLASPING THE HANDS OF ANGELS

In the middle of the night, flying over the ocean, snoring
beneath a cotton mask, dangling between the sea and the sky,

this is when I feel the angels hovering near.

They stir in the air outside the plane.

They curl up next to me in an empty seat,
humming lullabies and stirring memories of embryonic
floating, and primal baby life.

I sense the angels above, beside, and below us,

reaching up from the ocean depths, whispering reassurances,
clasping their wet hands with ours,

Wet,
warm,
slippery, familiar,

only to slide slowly away–

back down, down to the salt and
the silt.

Silencio

Descending
into the tomb of St. Francis—

a sign on the wall calls for "silencio."

Pilgrims wearing Nike shoes and Nautica shirts
file silently towards the crypt.

The heavy granite of the church above bears
down on us.

We circle deep in the earth around the remains of a

Saint.

Circling . . . circling.
The air sighs around us,
weary from holding the wishes, prayers, and thoughts
of all who have circled past this corpse.

And now, these wishes, prayers and hopes

hang above us,
slide down our shoulders,
and
melt
with our own

prayers
and
pleadings.

Our Lady of the Alley
The Animal and the Unknown

She is completely white–from the top of her veil to the
cracked pedestal she stands upon.

She stands with her hands resting at her sides, her palms
open.

A ring of roses rests at her feet. A browning daisy hangs
limply in the crook of her arm.

Her garden looks out on the alley.
Speed bumps grow out of the pavement, and blue metal
dumpsters guard garage doors.

Discarded televisions, end tables, sweatshirts,
fading photo albums, busted clocks, chairs with missing
legs,
radios with broken dials,
and children's shoes organize themselves on the
concrete pavement.

A woman with shafts of jutting grey hair, taped glasses,
three teeth missing, and garments laced with urine,
bacteria dying under her arms, and between her legs,

pushes a shopping cart along Mary's fence.

The wheels squeal.

This urban daughter pushes her cart, gazing intently over
her buggy's bulging surplus of pots and pans, winter coats,

army boots, stereo speakers, coffee grinders, cup holders, old cell phones, computer monitors, and television remote controls.

The wheels squeal and turn and yearn.
They sing to the Mother of God.

Mary listens intently, and receives this hymn of joy.

This hymn of joy-a hymn
to the animal and the unknown.

Rain

The rain washes over my face.

Dye drips from the flowers above me, pink,
green, blue, and yellow drops, drops
falling from the fabric flowers adorning my grave.

Spring must be arriving.

I only have seasons now, and quiet.

Quiet that envelopes all of us, sleeping here
with gentle comfort.

The Living run by, scattered by the rain,
seeking shelter.

But we, the dead, open our hands.

We know the rain brings creation.

We can feel life stirring,
stirring all around us,
as the ground drinks from the wet sky.

We no longer need to stir.

We know that our strength lies in stillness, in
the embrace of the earth, in the gentle giving of
the rain.

Memorial

I arrived home one evening in late November and there was a muted message on my answering machine. The voice, shocked and muffled, belonged to my friend Jimmy.

"Lisa, Linda's been murdered. I'm at the airport right now. I'll call you later when I get to Chicago."

Nothing made sense. Linda was Jimmy's ex-wife, a slight, lithe woman, with a kind heart and a touching innocence that belied her forty-plus years. Jimmy, an author, and I had become friends long after he and Linda had divorced. The two of them were still close friends, and their solid relationship was healthy and strengthening for their young daughter. I became a "friend of the family" and would join the divorced parents and daughter on dinner outings, weddings, and Jimmy's book signings.

When Jimmy finally arrived in Chicago, I learned that the Sunday after Thanksgiving, two men in hoods broke into Linda's apartment and stabbed her to death. Nothing made sense.

The next day, Jimmy called and asked if I would sing at the memorial service. I quickly agreed, because I wanted to help in any small way that I could. He asked me to sing one song at the beginning of the service and one at the end.

I woke up the morning of the service at 8:30 AM and lay in bed. I thought about Linda. My mind still couldn't comprehend the reality of what had taken place. I thought about the upcoming memorial service. In just six hours, I would be standing in front of stunned friends and family, and would be required to open my mouth and sing. I thought about Linda's face, her smile, her innocence. I thought of the church sanctuary. I thought of the carpeted steps leading up to the podium, where I would have to stand and sing. In my shock, would I even be able to make it up the steps without stumbling? I thought of the last time I'd seen Linda. I felt her embrace as we parted company. I thought of the five hundred people who would be staring at me at the beginning of the memorial service with grief and shock etched onto their faces. I looked at the clock. It was 8:46 AM. I continued to lie in bed, paralyzed with fear and grief.

At 2:15 PM, my fiancé Chris and I got into the blue-green Saturn. He stretched his long legs and settled into the driver's seat, looking over at me with kind, concerned eyes. I moved slowly as I settled into the seat and reached for the seat belt. I gripped Chris's hand as we drove the ten minutes to the church. I breathed in and out slowly, and yet continued to feel unsteady and distant from my inner core. We arrived at the church. Our car doors slammed, and I thought of Jimmy and his daughter. In my mind's eye, I saw Linda run up to me in the foyer of the Polish Catholic Church, white ribbons draped across the walls behind her, at the wedding we attended many months earlier. I struggled to bring myself back to the present moment, shaking my shoulders, and grabbing Chris's arm.

We entered Unity Church. It was packed with mourners in black. I suddenly saw Jimmy, and we threw our arms around each other in a painful yet comforting reunion.

I sat on the front row of the sanctuary. I stared at the ground and held tightly to Chris's hand. I still felt as if I was floating outside of my body. I looked at the clock. It was 2:54 PM. I would be singing in six minutes—but how? A group of pallbearers brought in the coffin. I stared at the white flowers that draped the coffin's lid. I couldn't move. How was I possibly going to sing?

I felt Chris's fingers interlocked with mine. Suddenly and unexpectedly, a deep peace began in my core and slowly moved through my body. This mysterious peace not only relaxed my arms, legs, shoulders, and chest, but also filled my mind. The tension that had filled my body and soul drifted away. I looked up slightly, focusing on my breath and struggling to comprehend what had just occurred in my being. A prayer of thanks flowed through my spirit. I squeezed Chris's hand and looked into his eyes.

"I'm going to be okay," I said. He put his arm around my shoulder.

The crowd grew quiet. I walked to the front, and looked out at hundreds of people. They looked back in grief, shock, and disbelief.

"Healer of our every ill, Light of each tomorrow," I sang.

"Give us peace beyond our fear and hope beyond our sorrow."

SMALL DIAMONDS

God has cast small diamonds from Her plane.
They have landed on the ground below
and have transformed themselves into
ponds, rivers, and streams that wink up at me as I fly by.
The river grows, and shimmers like a snake,
stretching out into the distance.
I watch this display,
as I teeter here on the edge of the infinite.
I vow to live my day "awake,"
and not take all for granted,
as God, sailing above in Her plane,
casts small diamonds down to me, that
settle in my soul,
and wink at all those beings
flying by.

At night, as I lay in bed,
the faces of the people on the bus, the train,
pass before my mind's eye.
I see them,
hoping, praying, wishing, incessantly talking on their
phones.
Planning, rushing, staring out the window.

We are all moving here, dancing here, assigned our own
special slice of space.

Our feet pound across the ground,
disturbing the insects who devour the earth below us,
and slither through their own special, tiny, tubular slice of
space.

We are all co-existing here as co-creators, co-beings,
whether mammal or shrubbery or fly.

The trees sway.
The branches reach skyward.
The grass turns green every spring.
The insects croak the songs the birds will
sing in the morning.
All of creation breathes the joy of life.

Breathes the joy of life, breathing, reaching,
singing—

not knowing how it came to
be, or where it is going.

LAUGHING GOD

Is it true?

Have our prayers been answered by
a rollicking, rambuctious God who
hides Herself, so we
can't hear Her laughter?

Who absorbs the steam of our
prayers and condenses them into

answers
that
baffle
and
confuse?

I labor on the shore, dear God—
earnestly building this boat, this
boat of my expectations.

I dream of sailing to the other side.

So why does She seem to shatter and obliterate my
boat as I begin my tour?

Leaving
me adrift.

Floating aimlessly with a board and a
nail?

I beg of you now—

Most Omnipotent Being, Great
Spirit, Yahweh, Jehovah, God of
Gods,
The Great I Am,
Who was—Who is—and Whoever
shall be—let me in on the joke!

The car door slams. I grasp for my bags, my
papers, my books.

I transform myself into the human camel. I teeter
towards my house.

Earl, late fifties, heavy–balding–smiling–
calls to me from his front steps–
once again holding court on North St. Louis.

He asks me about my day.
His warmth is relaxing, his interest is uplifting–as
it always is.

Two days later, the car door slams,

I grab the guitar, the tape player, the frayed, stray

newspapers, I teeter towards my house.
Earl calls.
He inquires, we laugh.

The sun is slowly disappearing.

Our talk is light and full of air.
He hesitates.
He talks of Vietnam, of his squadron,

of the orders they gave him–the children shot, the women
killed.

He says he still feels bad.
He tries not to think about it, but he does.

His words hang in the evening air. The sun is slowly
disappearing.

I leave my house Sunday morning.
I see Earl–dressed in a suit.
He is smiling.
We wave.

"Goin' to church?" he asks.
I say I am.

"Yeah," he says,
"me too."

Divine Spirit,
My body and soul have soaked in pools of confusion.

So many voices,
so many shouts of violent hatred have seeped into my skin.

The center of my being screams "No war anymore!"

But now there is someone before me–a brother–a sister–who
have themselves soaked in war.
Someone who has found themselves buried in skin to skin

battle, battle spawned by selfish political agendas.
The agendas of those who now sit quietly,
watching HD T.V. in freshly-vacuumed rooms.

I don't know what to ask you for, Divine Spirit,
I don't know how to organize this deep catastrophe within myself.

Hold me in my questioning.
Hold me, even when hope is elusive, and I am numb, sad, and
scared.

A Seat by the Window

Great Creator,
Thomas Merton once wrote,
"There is no way of telling people that they are all walking
around shining like the sun."

A few years ago, I observed a group of human beings
standing on the street corner, waiting for the bus, and I
was stunned by their beauty.

One of them held a plastic grocery bag of books and thrust
one thin hip out to the right. Another had a red scarf tied
tightly around her head, and dangled a polyester handbag.
She smiled into the air at nothing in particular.

A third royal creature pushed his bangs out of his eyes–and
fingered a perplexing pimple.

Through the lens of the ordinary, their beauty stunned
me–so distinct, full of fire, and endlessly creative.

All the forces of the universe–forces that have stirred and
bubbled throughout all of time had hurtled toward this
moment and shaped these three–and me.

Help me to see your cunning amazingness, Creator, in
every moment.

Every moment, as I stand among mountains climbing to
the sky,
and as I climb the steps of the bus, reach for my fare, and
hope for a seat by the window.

No one on this street seems to know who they
are.

Long before a human thought was formed

their essence brilliantly glimmered in the
womb of a galaxy
within the womb of a galaxy, within the
womb of a galaxy.

Their light—which now sits on a stoop, and
taps a foot to the beat—sped through the
interior eye of space and exploded
inconceivably into their
loping stride, their
turn of words, their
snorting laugh.

The mischievous spark that animates their fingers, their
toes, was once a boisterous giggle that popped forth from
the teetering infant
of the cosmos.

And now, and now, and now . . .

this same spark reaches for the newspaper on a front
porch
on Kedzie Avenue.

No one on this street seems to know who they are.

Or maybe they do.

Maybe they sense it–at times—

at times—when they awake at three in the morning,

suspended in the hidden holiness of night,

listening to the steady, calming rhythm of their lover's
breath, or

when a funeral procession slides around the corner,

and the shimmering fragility of life wraps around their
shoulders.

Maybe they feel it,
when the evening is soft and blessedly cool, and the city
seems quiet—almost still, and the hypnotic throbbing of
God beats in the pavement.

Holy One, grant us the grace to celebrate the mystery of every step,
to live in wonder and gratitude for all that is above our reach.

During my two years at St. Catherine's Catholic Worker, the events of death and resurrection took on new meaning for me. Through the gift of grace, I experienced not only the resurrections of our guests, but also my own resurrections. Much of what I encountered seemed to reveal to me radiant shadows of who we really are, and how what is "above our reach" can often help us through the slaps and submergence of loss and seeming despair.

One such experience is etched clearly in my memory. It was a day in March, 1991; I was touring the east coast with *Haunted by God: The Life of Dorothy Day*. I was staying in a retreat center in New Jersey, and one evening, at around 10:30, after everyone else had gone to bed, I sat in a "closet-turned-phone-booth" and called home. Joseph was on duty that night. He answered the phone, and as he gave me the general "house news," I heard Dave, one of the other Catholic workers, asking to speak to me. He got on the phone and simply said, "Rick died this afternoon." I was silent. Suddenly, I felt very far away. "I thought you'd want to know," he continued, "'cause I know you felt close to him."

"Thanks, Dave."

I hung up the phone, sat in the phone booth, and cried. I felt bewildered and alone. Everyone was asleep. Should I wake someone up? Should I call someone? I wandered out of the booth, found my way to the chapel, and sat numbly in a chair in front of the altar.

Finally, I went back upstairs. I had a show the next day, which I decided to dedicate to Rick. I thought about how Rick had sat on the front row at one of my performances in Chicago. He saw the play before we had added music and made revisions. He always wanted to see the new version—I guess now he'd have a chance.

Rick Henry Anderson moved into St. Catherine's in October of 1990. I always thought he looked a little like De Niro, though no one else seemed to agree. Rick quickly won us over with his warmth and friendly disposition. He was very affirming and let you know that he enjoyed your company. At Halloween, I dressed up as Doris Day—complete with an evening gown and bouffant wig. Rick wore a black beret, sunglasses, and a red scarf around his neck, and went as my agent. The roles stuck, and from then on, whenever I saw Rick, I would ask him if he'd gotten any work for me.

"Oh yeah," he would say. "I'm workin' on a film deal right now with Swayze."

"Well let me know, Rick. I need the money."

"Sure."

One bright afternoon, as I descended from our neighborhood train platform, I spotted Rick walking home. He was coming back from class. He talked about how he was studying to be a drug rehab counselor. We talked all the way home. I don't remember much about the conversation, but I remember the sound of Rick's laughter, and the distinct sense of calm I felt in his presence.

In December, Rick moved to Bonaventure House, a home for

people living with AIDS on the north side of Chicago. Bonaventure was a beautiful new facility with a loving and caring staff. We were all happy for him.

After his move, I saw Rick less frequently, but I always had him in the back of my mind and tried to get over to Bonaventure whenever I could. When a visit was possible, I would call and tell him I was coming. When I would arrive, he would be waiting in the front lobby. We would sit at one of the round dining room tables, drink RC, and catch up, often telling stories about our lives. And, of course, we would go back to the old "routine."

"Got any work for me, Rick?"

"Sure, I'm workin' on a really hot deal with Pacino."

"Well, let me know. I need the money, man."

As I lay in my bed in New Jersey, these memories washing over me, I remembered the last time I went to visit Rick. Though I had called ahead of time, he failed to meet me at the front door. One of the staff helped me find him. We discovered him in the rec room puzzling over a fish tank. For months, he had gloried in taking care of the five-foot-wide tank of tropical fish. When I walked in the room, he looked at me drunkenly and said, "Hello, baby." He had never flirted with me before and his tone jarred me.

I began to study his rec room project. He had removed the white rocks from the bottom of the fish tank, rinsed them, and then placed them once again in the tank of water. The fish had been temporarily removed, and placed to the side in a large bowl of water for this project. He swaggered about the tank. I was growing concerned, and shared nervous glances with the staff member. Both of us seemed bewildered as to how we should respond. Rick began placing the blue, red, and orange fish back in the huge tank of water. Shaken and speechless, we watched as each fish swam for a few seconds, froze in the tank, and then floated silently to the surface. The staff person gently asked Rick how he had cleaned the rocks. "With bleach," Rick answered. The fish continued to die. Dementia had gripped him. He had entered the end stages of AIDS.

And now, he was dead.

Thankfully, I made it to Rick's funeral. My 747 landed at O'Hare at ten o'clock in the morning, and I jumped into a cab with a struggling purple flower someone had given me after a show that weekend. I made it to the ceremony five minutes before the opening prayer. I was fortunate to meet some of Rick's family members. They seemed grateful when I told them how much Rick had meant to all of us at St. Catherine's.

In my heart, I knew that Rick was resurrected. I knew that he had crossed over, and I would see him again. But I felt the unreality and heaviness of grief, and I missed him. I thought about all of our guests who had died. I felt as though an angry dark mist hung about me. I was experiencing my own "death."

I left the funeral and proceeded with life as usual. I traveled to Esperanza Community Services to teach my Wednesday theatre class to adults with developmental disabilities. As I drove along Lake Shore Drive, pulled onto I-55, and headed to the school, I sensed my sadness and grief transforming into disillusionment and self-pity. I let go, and let the dark feelings take over my spirit.

I was relieved upon my arrival at school to find only two students could attend class that day. Despite my state of mind, class seemed to go well, though a dense cloud still hung about me. We were beginning the "Hat Game," when Bobby Tirelli brought out his tape recorder and said, "After this, I am going to play this tape—and we will dance." Bobby is a plump, tall, jovial Italian man with mischievous, huge brown eyes and a balding head. I told Bobby that we could definitely dance—after we finished—no problem.

After we completed our game, he got an excited look on his face. He cleared some metal folding chairs out of the way, set up his tape recorder, and sat in a chair facing me. He flung his right hand dramatically in the air and solemnly pressed the "play" button.

Gently and imperceptibly, the overture to Electric Light Orchestra's "Can't Get It Out of My Head" began to fill the classroom. Bobby held his hands up in front of his chest and closed his eyes—indicating to me that we were not to dance at this point—but we were to simply absorb the music that was circling around us. The tones and chords swept around the room. Bobby kept his eyes closed and breathed in every note. Finally, the overture subsided and the unmistakable, clear tenor of Jeff Lynne slid into the air. Bobby Tirelli opened his eyes, looked at me, held out his hand and announced, "Now, we dance."

I rose from my seat and whirled around the room with Bobby as the music whirred around us. We spun in circles. We twirled and dipped. The heaviness began to drop off of my shoulders and onto the floor. Bobby laughed and concentrated very hard on his steps. I spun in circles. I laughed . . . I sang with the music . . . I felt the sun on my face . . . I felt resurrection rising up within me. And in Bobby's eyes, in the music, in the sunlight, and in the dance—I am certain I heard Rick Henry Anderson, laughing.

Holy One, grant us the grace to celebrate the mystery of every step, to live in wonder and gratitude for all that is above our reach.

ALONG

"I love you, you love me, we're all a part of God's body,
Stand with me . . . I need you to survive."

Andrea, a thirty-seven-year-old woman with compassionate eyes and smooth brown skin, stood on the chapel stage of the state correctional center singing these words, written by composer Hezekiah Walker. It was the second performance of an original play, Phenomenal Women: Our Past Does Not Reflect Our Future, *created by nine incarcerated women. Andrea sang, looking into the eyes of her fellow inmates, who sat in the audience on wooden pews. She looked at them with deep love, offering the gift of herself.*

"We're all a part of God's body . . ."

Our lives are entirely about relationships—not only relationships with other human beings, but with all creation. My breath moves in and out, in constant conversation with the air. I walk along with others, often by choice, and often not, feeling challenged and threatened by them, but also sharing love, reveling in shared joy, and working through anger. Through my work with women in prison, leading theatre and writing workshops for Still Point Theatre Collective, I've often witnessed the complexities of the relational labyrinth. I've listened to women speak of their despair at being separated from their children. I've watched liberating relationships grow and prosper in an environment that is anti-liberation. In the prison environment, jailers and the jailed walk along with each other. They are thrust into relationships that are not of their choosing, and yet, surprisingly, growth and compassion not only survive, but often rise up and flourish.

Years ago, a group of women at the state correctional center stunned me with their compassion. They inspired me with their loving response to tragedy.

"We really experienced a lot of unity here," Lana's voice moved across the phone lines. Lana was my administrative contact at the state correctional center in central Illinois where I taught a weekly theatre and writing workshop. They experienced unity. She was referring to the officers, staff, and inmates of the facility.

I thought back to the previous Monday. Nine of us sat in the solarium, a room with windows all around and red stone tiles on the floor. We could hear the echoing voices of the women in the housing unit next door. Their shouts and laughter penetrated the windows and reverberated off the walls. In the adjoining hallway, a copy machine hummed and slapped. We were doing our usual "check in" at the beginning of class, going around the circle and listening to each woman, to find out who was sad, who was feeling good, or who had just had a visit from a friend or relative.

We came to one of the last women in the circle, Lee, a tall, lithe woman with kind eyes and mocha skin. She looked aghast at the group and said, "I can't believe no one has mentioned the tragedy. An officer was killed last Thursday."

I caught my breath. The first thing I thought of was prison violence, but she continued, "He was leaving work on his motorcycle last Thursday night, and some woman hit him on the highway—right in front of the prison."

Monique shook her head,

"Yeah, and he had a wife and three babies at home."

A quiet filled the solarium.

"He was never that friendly to me," Lee continued, "but that morning, the morning of the day he died, he was messin' with me. He was jokin' around with me, for the first time. And then, just a few hours later, he was dead."

"We know they had a memorial," Rosie offered, "and we really wanted his family to know how sorry we were."

Lee added, "Some women were bein' nasty about it, but we told them to shut it."

The ten of us sat in the quiet, the air pulled taut as we honored the memory of the officer with our unbidden, spontaneous silence. Only the shouts of the women in the adjoining unit sliced through the air.

As I walked back to the gate house after class, I contemplated the grief that was shared and prayed for the family of the officer. I marveled, with humility and awe, at this group of incarcerated women, deeply mourning the loss of one of their jailers.

Holy One, guide us as we walk along with each other, and all of creation. Offer us a salve for our anger and grief, and a safe place for our liberating love.

COME BACK

In praise of St. Catherine's Catholic Worker, offering hospitality for men and women living with AIDS and HIV, Chicago, Illinois, 1989–1998

Faces, passing before me—laughing eyes, gnarly hands,
hair—brown—hair—nappy—hair—blonde, dyed.

Arms and legs–tracks on arms, a cane to walk–a body
jammed between bed and wall—body—fainting, screaming.

Joy—arms to embrace at the door.
faces—welcoming—hands—applauding—
food and conversation, Come back, come back.

Parties—no alcohol
parties—more food—loose talk—
"Damn, Lisa, you've had a boring life.
You'd have made a great hooker and drug addict."
Photographs—mouths open in exultation.
Arms flailing—Come back, come back.

Movies, trips in the green Buick.
Finally away, finally alone—
"Have I made a difference to you?" No answer.
Tears from the asked—happy surprise, Come back.

Windows, open—blue blanket
clinging in the summer, large eyes,
thinning body—Staring eyes,
endless television,
"If people just made love," he says,
"The world would be a better place."

Screams of grief—one thirty A.M.—
holding each other—folding the blue
blanket—wiping each other's eyes,
unity.

The storm subsides.
Little jokes, laughter of relief, to
bed at 4:30 or 5. Come back.

Faces—circling—
sometimes returning—
Faces sometimes circling away—
away—
only left in memory—in Spirit.

Songs and psalms chosen carefully.
Bodies still in coffins.
Beloved faces, all, all around,

Tacky lobbies, gold fish and
funerals.
A body left—
left for two weeks—
embalmed, ready,
but no money to be found.
"It's business," they say.

A courtyard of green with St.
Francis staring through glass eyes.

Holy One, Demanding Parent, I am so afraid to grow.

So many times in the past, growth has meant pain.
Stretching–stretching that pulls me so taut–that I feel I
will crack open.

Holy One, growth does not happen in isolation.
Growth erupts in relationships, in relationships with
"the others" you have placed in my life.

"The others"—a friend, a lover, a comrade,
these individuals–bring bursts of light into my life—but
also show me myself.

This showing can be full of wonder and awe—but also
full of
horror and disappointment as my smoldering, struggling
self is revealed. Interests and perspectives clash, and I am
left sad and disillusioned. I claw and wound the ones I love
the most.

If I run, I shun growth; I continue in my old matrix,
force a strained smile,
and blissfully live in painful illusion.

But if I allow myself to dive deep, below the surface,
thrashing wildly, yet safely within the realm of love,

perhaps I can emerge, emerge from this tar-like pond,
maybe drenched, maybe with my hair sticking to my head,
but more whole, more illuminated,
as the sun of love dries my soaking skin, and gently pats
dry my humbled and healthier soul.

Niño

For the little boy I saw on a bench in an impoverished village in El Salvador in 1994.

Oh Niño,
I saw you sitting on the bench,
naked and covered with dust.

Your soul sitting there, bore a hole in my
spirit, a hole as dusty and naked as you.

Oh Niño,
Your eyes were so wide as you watched the
show, but you didn't smile, Niño, only
looked–wide and innocent.

I wanted to touch you, to give you clothes,
to give you warmth.
I wanted to push down your bulging tummy
and make you feel peaceful, whole.

But
I
didn't.

I looked at you, and saw that you were
surrounded by thousands of Niños.

I didn't feel helpless. I didn't feel angry.

I felt something new and dark, something

so new that I hadn't words to define it,

and so dark that though I squinted my eyes,
I couldn't see it.

I left your side.
I drove away in a cloud of dust.
I rattled past the huts covered with grasses.
I wondered which one of them was yours, Niño,

and then I realized that they all were.

Niño,
I had a hard day today.
My flight was late and I was frustrated and
angry.

My bags were heavy, Niño. My side hurts.
I have just finished my dinner, Niño.
The chicken was good and the brownie

finished off the meal nicely,

nicely,

nicely.

I can see you, Niño, sitting on the bench,
naked, eyes wide, coated with dust.

The hole that you bore in my spirit is filled
with your eyes, with your bulging stomach.

You will be with me again and again,
as I
take my bath,
ride the train,
brush my teeth.

You will speak to me when I sleep.

Please Niño,

please never,

never

leave.

AUNT RUTH

When I was a child,
my Aunt Ruth was a magical person.

She was in her mid-eighties,
and constantly traveled around the country, on
Greyhound buses.

My father would announce that
Aunt Ruth was coming for a visit,
and would set forth for the Greyhound station.

She would arrive in a frumpy flowered dress with wire-
rimmed spectacles and a crazy, inventive hat.
Her gray hair would be smashed beneath her chapeau,
struggling to break free.

She was always delighted to see us,
and would look at us with wonder and reverence,
gasping at "how much we had grown."

She would always take pictures,
and laugh with her hand covering her mouth.

The magic would last for a few hours, or an
evening, or a night–and into the morning, and
then she would be back in the car, my father at
the helm,
sallying forth towards the Greyhound station.

Aunt Ruth had wanted to be a missionary when she was

a young woman, back in the 1920s,
but they told her "no," that women weren't missionaries,
and gave her a desk job.

But–she showed them.

At the age of fifty,

she became a Methodist minister, and on
her eightieth birthday,
she traveled to China.

I often wonder if she got there on a Greyhound bus.

Yabba Dabba Doo Alleluia

Eddy—a forty-five-year-old man with a
developmental disability, sits in my theater
class.

He still wears his brown jacket, though I've
asked him to remove it.

He sits —
with a Buddha-like half smile on his lips,
gazing slightly downward.

In his right hand he holds a Fred Flintstone
doll, brought in to use as a prop in our
Christmas play.

Eddy has decided that Fred Flintstone will
play the baby Jesus.

I trust his choice.

So, Fred will be wrapped in swaddling clothes,
and placed in a manger,
because there is no room for him in the inn.

Yabba dabba doo, dabba doo, alleluia.

I passed beneath the fluorescent lights, across the square green tiles and found my bleary-eyed way to the office workroom. With only a murmur of enthusiasm, I folded the fundraising letters, which had just emerged fresh from the copy machine. The workroom was quiet. The halls were silent. My co-workers had long submerged themselves in Chicago's rush-hour traffic, and left me alone. Around ten o'clock P.M., I finally put my key in the security lock and headed out the back door of the building that housed my theatre office. With a tinge of relief and resentment, I dropped the fundraising letters in the corner mailbox. One of the letters was addressed to Monsignor Jack Egan.

I had met Jack many years before following a performance of my one-woman play *Haunted by God* on the life of Catholic activist Dorothy Day. Dorothy had cofounded the Catholic Worker movement, which had developed into a network of houses of hospitality for homeless people scattered across the United States and overseas. That night, I was performing on a small stage in a former Catholic high school. Jack approached me immediately following the performance. He was a short, balding, elderly man with wire-rimmed spectacles, a roman collar, a glowing smile, and a relentless twinkle in his eye. He gave me a meaty handshake and said, "Wonderful, wonderful."

Later, as I was packing my stage props, one of my co-playwrights, Bob McClory, a former priest-turned-journalism-professor, informed me that I had just met the legendary Jack Egan. He said that Jack had dedicated his life to the fight for social justice. As we left the building, Bob gave me a brief synopsis of his life. Jack had spent decades fighting for fair housing for the city's marginalized people. He fought the expansion of the University of Chicago in the 1950s, going "head to head" against Mayor Daley. Jack was moved to fight because he knew the expansion would displace many struggling, low-income people. Later, he headed up the office of Urban Affairs for the Archdiocese of Chicago where he opposed the warehousing of poor families and fought corrupt real estate agents. In 1965, he marched with Dr. King, and inspired clergymen across the country to join the civil rights movement. At the time I was thankful to learn Jack's story. Now, years later, remembering my first and only encounter with him, I mailed the funding request, hoping he would remember me and make a contribution.

A week later, as I stared at my archeological layers of papers, envelopes, post-it notes, and Catholic holy cards piled on top of my desk, the mail arrived. I received a check from Jack for $75. Along with the check was a short note, typed on a half-sheet of paper. It read, "Don't give up, beautiful woman. It's hard on artists these days." Then he added, "Let's have lunch some time." I was intrigued by his lunch invitation, but I was leaving town for a two-month European tour, and was unable to respond. A year later, I sent him another funding request. A week passed, and I received another $75 and another typed note that, once again, ended with "Let's have lunch some time." I read this second lunch invitation, placed the note on top of the papers, envelopes, post-it notes, and Catholic holy cards, and thought, "Am I crazy? How could I pass up a chance to have lunch with this man?" I immediately found the phone and called his office. I spoke with his long-time administrative assistant and comrade, Peggy Roach, and scheduled a lunch date with Jack.

Two days later, the two of us were walking arm in arm down Michigan Avenue, heading to his favorite lunch spot. People were rushing past us in all directions, but we merely strolled down the sidewalk, he in his roman collar and I in my perpetual skirt. He looked over at me and said, "We've met once or twice, haven't we?" Twenty minutes later, sitting in a restaurant overlooking Lake Michigan, our elbows resting on a linen tablecloth, Jack looked at me and said, "Tell me the story of your life."

This first lunch date was followed by many others. We would talk endlessly over chicken and salad or cashew shrimp and egg rolls.

He would say, "How is your work going?" I would vent. He would offer advice.

He would say, "How can I help you?"

I would reply, "Jack, just continue to listen to me." He was indignant.

"Oh, I'm sure you have plenty of people who can do that for you."

Determined to help in a tangible way, he became passionate about featuring my one-woman play on Dorothy Day at Holy Name Cathedral. Holy Name, a towering Gothic cathedral in the heart of downtown Chicago, was Jack's current residence. He arranged a meeting between me and the pastor of the Cathedral, Bob McLaughlin, a kind white-haired man with a welcoming smile. The meeting day arrived. Jack sat regally in a brown leather chair in his priest's residence. He proudly introduced the pastor and me and stated, "I want to do her show here, and her company is to keep all of the revenues." With great love and admiration, Bob looked at Jack and said, "Of course."

Two months before the performance, I left Jack a phone message. My words were rushed and tumbled blindly over themselves. "Jack, the show is coming up. Should I send out bulletin announcements? Should I call the papers? Should I make a flier? Should I call the radio stations? Jack, call me, and tell me what I should do." The next day, I received Jack's simple reply on my voice mail. "This is Monsignor Jack Egan for Lisa Wagner. I just want to tell her that I love her," and he hung up.

In spite of my worries, two hundred people came to the cathedral performance. Jack stood up in front of the crowd to introduce me, and momentarily blanked on my name. He quickly referenced his notes. The audience laughed good-naturedly. They continued to laugh throughout the performance in all the appropriate places and walked closely with me through the silences. Applause and laughter filled the hall. After the show, Jack was aglow. "A great day," he said, grasping my hand, "A great day."

In the winter of 2001, Jack's health began to fail. He was now eighty-four years old, and his heart was fading. It became harder for me to see him since he had very little strength and was in and out of the hospital. I sent him a hand-written note on a blue-flowered card, "I'm praying for you Jack. I hope to see you soon." Finally, one day, we spoke on the phone and made a plan to see each other on a Saturday morning at eleven o'clock. Before we hung up, Jack said, "Be sure to call first, because my health has been 'up and down' and if I'm having a bad day, I might not be able to see you."

The day arrived, and in my excitement to see Jack, I forgot to call. I took the train to Holy Name Cathedral. The receptionist for the priests' residence was a baby-faced seminarian. I asked if I could see the Monsignor. We rode the ancient elevator to Jack's quarters, and the seminarian told me that my visit would have to be brief, since my friend wasn't feeling well. I walked into his study. He was sitting in his leather armchair in front of the window, the tall buildings rising up behind him, surrounded by books. We greeted each other, and I sat next to him.

"I was doing so well," he said, tightening his fist for emphasis, "Then I got this cold, and I've been going downhill ever since." He paused and looked at me, "I'm about ready to give up."

He folded his hands and a smile slowly crossed his face. He sighed and said, "I'll never forget that show we did here at the cathedral. A great day. A great day."

He began to fish through his books. "I have a holy card of Doro-thy Day that I'd like to give to you." He searched and searched. Still unable to find the card, he leafed through a beige book with gold writing embossed on the cover. "Have you seen this? It's *Sonnets to the Unseen*. It's a book of reflections on the life of Christ. You can use it for prayer or meditation." He gave me the book. I looked it over and began to hand it back to him. He pushed it back and said, "No, keep it."

It was now time for me to leave. Jack took both of my hands in his and kissed them. I departed.

I stayed in the neighborhood for a long time. I sat on a hard wooden pew in the cathedral and then wandered across the street and lingered in a coffee shop. I sat silently. My body felt light. My movements were few and slow. My thoughts were quiet and meandered solemnly around Jack.

A week later, on a Sunday afternoon, I drove to Mundelein, Illinois to visit some friends. We sat in the living room, as shafts of sunlight played across the floor. "That's sad about Jack Egan," one of them said. "They announced at mass this morning that he died yesterday."

After I returned home, I leafed through the book Jack had given to me, *Sonnets to the Unseen*. Out of one hundred and ninety-six pages, only one page had a corner turned down. The sonnet on this page was about the crucifixion, and reflected on the two thieves who hung on crosses to the right and left of Jesus. One thief taunts Jesus, "Save yourself and us." The second thief silences the first. He knows he will soon die. He asks Jesus, "When you come into your Kingdom, remember me." Jesus simply replies, "Today, you will be with me in Paradise."

I placed my orange tray on the round white table in the mother-house dining room. The room was huge, with brown tiled floors and a high, beige ceiling. I was doing *Haunted by God: The Life of Dorothy Day* for this community of sisters.

I looked at my food: a salad in a toffee-colored plastic bowl, a white plate with chicken fried steak coated with brown gravy, a puffy roll, and a vegetable medley of diced peas, carrots, and potatoes.

I grasped my glass of water, took a drink, and, as I placed the glass back on the tray, I caught sight of a tall, dark figure entering the cafeteria. She wore a long, black traditional habit that flowed to the floor and firmly gripped her pale face at the top. Her ears and neck were completely covered—only her face peeked out. Her chin and cheeks were monstrously thin and drawn. They matched her skeleton-like hands that protruded from the ends of her long, black arms. I guessed that she must be at least one-hundred-and-thirty years old.

I looked down at my plate as she made her way to the buffet. Deep within myself, I said an earnest prayer: "Please, please, God, don't let her sit with me."

A few minutes passed. I worked through my food slowly as I wrestled with my feelings, smiling and nodding at the other diners as they passed me. I remembered stories I had heard from some of my friends who had attended Catholic schools. The ste-reotypes they described did not resonate with my own, amazing encounters with incredible Catholic sisters. I let out a sigh, and

I tried to see this sister in a different light. I overheard someone at the next table talking about the new movie *Shakespeare in Love*. I reached for my napkin. Suddenly, I felt a presence hovering close. My muscles tightened. I glanced to my right. She was there. She was unmistakable with her chiseled face and sweeping black garment. She spoke. "May I join you?"

"Yes," I said, forcing a smile.

She sat down, unfolded her napkin, and grinned at me. We began to talk, and she introduced herself as Sister Mary Agnes. As we conversed, the dark figure I had feared began to transform. She became kind, animated, intelligent, and thoughtful. Her thin face was now glowing with warmth and care.

As our conversation progressed, she began to talk of her longtime work with ecumenism, struggling to bring together the different Christian churches. She described an upcoming ecumenical meeting she was organizing.

"How did you get involved with this?" I asked her.

She smiled and blushed.

"Well, it goes back a ways."

I tilted my head with curiosity.

"Well, when I was a young girl, maybe seventeen, I had a boyfriend. I really, really cared for him."

She took an ice cube out of her water glass and put it in her black tea, to cool it down.

"He was very handsome."

She leaned towards me.

"I remember once, he took me to the carnival, and we went up on the Ferris wheel." She paused, and thoughtfully folded her napkin, smoothing the folds.

"And I'll never forget it, but when we were up there, we were sitting so close, and he reached over and put his arm around my waist."

She gently curved her hand, wrist, and elbow in a soft letter "C" to demonstrate.

"But you see, he was Presbyterian, and I, of course, was Catholic. So, I couldn't marry him. Though I know he really did love me."

"What happened?" I asked.

"When I left high school, I joined the sisters. I felt I had a vocation."

"And what happened to him?"

"He went to college and then got married."

She shrugged and pushed her vegetable medley to the side of her plate. A smile came across her face, and she looked at me. She lowered her voice.

"He did come back to see me, though, a few years ago. His wife had died, and he came here to the motherhouse. We talked for a while. I felt like maybe he was hoping for something—I don't know—but I just couldn't leave."

I nodded, without saying a word.

We sat for a few moments in the silence. In the quiet, I thought of her, sitting on a Ferris wheel, whirling upward and down again, laughing with a handsome young man, a warm, tender arm tucked snuggly around her waist.

HALF LIFE

In that half-life between waking and dreaming, your
memory brushes softly against my mind,

discovering me in my vulnerable state,
defenses diminished,
dreaming of stone-like children and
animals
toppled over in village streets.

Last night, I had vowed to forget you–to make a new,
anguished start.

But now, in this half-life between waking and dreaming,
I embrace you,
and know in my release,
that I will awaken
in another half-life–
between waking and dreaming,
and you will be lying at my side

LITTLE WILLY

I remember the living room,

gathering the neighbor kids from the four corners of my
block—sitting them down on the cushy white sofas—their
short legs dangling—
placing the 45 of "Little Willy Willy" on the stereo
turntable—and dancing around the room, between the
grand piano and the Hi-Fi, moving my lips to the words
of the song—always striving to entertain.

Years later, I sat up late one night, singing "Little Willy
Willy" in the dark.
You sang with me, your hand resting on mine.

I was almost forty now, but once again, childlike and
innocent.

Warm as a candle,
transforming itself through fire and fluidity
is my love for you.
The wax obediently abandons its
solid state,
and runs downward,
only to become solid again–
with a new shape, a new form,
transformed by the intention of the Universe.
Fire melts wax.

The Universe
speaks to me of birth in every second.
Birth into love–zygote, embryo, fetus.
Love is coaxing me to grow, to be
transformed.

Let my unformed mass curl into hands,
toes, lips, skull.
Where there was nothing, let a new bond shine.

A new bond,
warm as a candle,

transforming itself
through fire and
fluidity.

THE BREATH OF GOD

We lay in our bed on a frozen January morning,
soft cotton, t-shirts, pajama pants, arms, legs—
entwined in a primal, infant-like embrace.

The mystery of our love has carried us here.

The harsh wind blows outside—blows against the
window, the bricks—

and you and I—our bodies entwined—

are like the breath of God—
steamy and warm—
hanging in the air on a cold day.

My friend Mary's daughter, Annie, twenty-three months
old, was born profoundly disabled.

She has a long, thin body that is stretched out and rigid.
She has a distended head with tiny wisps of soft, brown
hair.
Saliva runs from her tiny lips
and she looks at you with beautiful, wide-open eyes.

When my husband Chris and I went to visit my parents in
Kansas City,
Mary and Annie came over for a potluck dinner.
They brought potato chips, 7-Up, and pasta to contribute
to the meal.
Mary gently laid Annie on her blankets in the living room
so she could sit down and eat—
sit down and eat for just a few moments.

After a few minutes went by,
Chris volunteered to bring Annie to the table. He walked to
her side.
He kneeled down, folding up his six-foot frame,
and softly wrapped her in a pink and white blanket. He
lifted her in his arms.
He slowly walked back to the table,
sat down and gently cradled her stretched out body.
She looked up at him with her wide beautiful eyes–and he
looked back.
She drooled and bit her lip.

He wiped her lip with a square white towel. She let out a small, contented sound.

He looked at her. He looked at me.

He is the last person I kissed.

In my twenties, I lived with an elderly German woman,
Hanni Haase. With age, her body and mind had become
sluggish and slow.

Every morning, I would brush her long, white hair and
sing the folk song "The Water is Wide."
I found this "one on one" time soothing and peaceful.

Together, we would discover stillness while performing a
seemingly mundane task.

After living together for a year, Hanni's health began to
deteriorate. One morning,
I helped her into the dining room to perform our brushing
ritual.
I placed my hands on her temples, and discovered that
they had sunken in.

At that moment, I knew she was going to die.

I put down the hair brush, and knelt beside her.
I put my arms around her,
and she leaned her head against my shoulder.

We sat there for a long time, in this peaceful embrace.
I don't remember how long we sat there, but she didn't let
go until I did.

We stood around Matthew's bedside. Five of us, all workers at St. Catherine's Catholic Worker, kept watch as Matthew struggled through his last hours. Matthew had been a much-loved member of our community for many years. He had large brown eyes and a soft, gentle spirit. Dave had agreed to walk with Matthew through his end stages, and a beautiful bond had formed between them. But at this moment, when Matthew was so close to death, Dave was somewhere out in the city, yet hopefully heading home. I touched the side of Matthew's bed, and looked at him, his eyes closed, resting against a white pillow case.

I remembered a visit to the hospital several months before. I arrived on his hospital floor feeling deeply agitated. I had just spent several minutes fighting traffic, and I was frustrated and angry. Now, I arrived at Cook County hospital and made my way through the AIDS ward. The ward was partitioned off by white curtains. I found Matthew in a small seven-by-five-foot area, bordered by the white curtains. When he saw me, he pulled himself up and sat on the edge of the bed. He was wearing a blue and white hospital gown. I sat in a stray orange vinyl chair in his "room." That week, Matthew had been at the edge of death, but he had made an incredible recovery. He was feeling deeply grateful, "God is good," he said.

I thought about the traffic jam and my deep anger. Matthew's peacefulness and gratitude embraced my being. "God is good," he said again. I slowly nodded in agreement. We continued to talk, and he said that the doctors were predicting that he would be in the hospital for at least a couple more weeks.

"It can be so boring," he said.

I asked him if he ever journaled. He said that he hadn't, but he was interested in writing. "I'll get you a journal; maybe that would help."

The next week, another one of the workers went to see Matthew. I gave her a simple red spiral notebook to give to him.

And now, five months later, we stood around Matthew's bed. His breath grew shallower and shallower. Finally, Dave returned. His thin frame created a shadow in the doorway. He pushed up his glasses and entered the room. He glanced at our worried faces. We stepped back to allow him to come to Matthew's side. He approached slowly, drew in a deep breath, and then climbed onto the bed next to Matthew. He lay with him for a moment. He kissed his cheek, and said, "It's okay, Matthew. It's time to go to Jesus now."

Within moments, Matthew slipped away. We cried, held each other, and prayed the Lord's Prayer around his bed.

After an hour of holding vigil, I sorrowfully left the house and drove to the north side of Chicago for a meeting. That evening, I returned home. The undertakers had come for Matthew, and Dave was cleaning his room. I went to check on him. When I walked in the room, Dave said, "I know I don't have to do this right now, but I have to do something."

He looked at me steadily, paused, and reached into an open drawer, "Actually, I have something for you."

He brought out the red spiral notebook I had given to Matthew.

He opened it to the first page. "I thought you might like to have this." He tore out the page and handed it to me. It was a letter.

"Dear Lisa, Thank you for your love and true concern. I was looking for something to do while I recovered from sickness, and you suggested the ideal thing. For this, your love for people, especially with this illness, deserves deep appreciation and love in return. Sincerely, your friend, Matthew Lewis."

Holy One, guide us as we walk along with each other, and all of creation. Offer us a salve for our anger and grief and a safe place for our liberating love.

INSIDE

When I was five years old, I used to sit in the backseat of our family car and gaze up and out of the window. I would watch the tops of the trees and the gargoyles perched on the rooftops of passing buildings and gaze at the white clouds—shaped like lambs, balloons, or squirrels with acorns. When it rained, I would watch the droplets form at the top of the window and scoot their way down the glass—hundreds of them—almost identical—swimming to their downward destination. Watching this display, I felt a strange sense of comfort. The rain was soothing and contemplative. Now, as an adult, I still watch the drops of rain on car windows, and this strange sense of comfort is awakened once again. As I have gotten older, rain has continued to draw me inside, to draw me within.

On a rainy day five years ago, after a full day of running around, I pulled my blue-green Saturn into a downtown parking space. I turned off the radio, windshield wipers, and ignition. I was reaching for the door handle when my eye was caught by hypnotic steady drops of rain splashing in a puddle. I caught my breath, leaned back in the seat, and just watched. As I meditated on the glistening puddle and listened to the rain on the roof of the car, I said a prayer and breathed deeply. I breathed within the silent expansive space between the raindrops and the wet black pavement.

Years earlier, in my late twenties, I went on a retreat in the Pacific Northwest. Needless to say, it rains quite a bit in that region of the country, so I had plenty of opportunities to meditate with the rain. For my retreat, I was staying at the L'Arche prayer house, Hopespring, in Tacoma, Washington. I was taking three

months out from my life to journal, pray, and basically attempt to ground myself in the essential call of my life. One evening, I found myself alone in the house. I made a cup of orange tea and sat in the sunroom. It was around seven in the evening and was growing dark outside. Storm clouds began to gather, blocking out the sun. Slowly, the rain began to fall, only a few drops at first, but then a soothing steady stream of drops began to cascade from the sky.

I sat in the dark as the rain danced around every side of the sunroom. The rhythmic sound of the rain plunged me deep into my spirit, deep into a divine peacefulness. In the middle of this dance, I could hear one solitary wind chime that hung from a beam outside, dancing back and forth, pulled to and fro by the rain and the wind. I sat transfixed, awestruck by the rain, the thunder, the wind, and the steady, solid voice of the chime. This accidental symphony drew me deep within, drew me home.

Holy One, thank you for the accidental symphonies that waft into our lives and draw us deep within, draw us home.

DIVINE MOTHER

In the shell of myself,

there lives a young girl,

soft-faced, questioning, flat
breasted, hair flying.

She sees herself falsely, ugly,
clumsy,
big-nosed and interrupting.

She still clamors inside of me,

fussing with her hair, wondering
about her weight.

And then there is me—now—walking
about, nearing forty, fearful still, not
knowing who I
am.

Seeing myself falsely,

overweight, unintelligent, confused, a
failure.

I clamor about myself—

doubting my gifts, second-guessing,
afraid.

And yet, in the midst of the clamoring, I

can see—

in the shell of myself,

a very old, very
wise woman
emerging from the shadows.

She slowly inhales, slowly exhales—
calming the child and the woman,

singing ancient, familiar songs,
songs of dream and spirit,
songs that seduce the clamoring fears into submission.

Her worn hands,
wrinkled with years that the
child
and the woman have not known,

gently soothe.

But it is her eyes—

dark,

gentle,

two shining stones,

that embrace us with a love
that knew no genesis,

a love that has simply always been.

The Divine Mother holds us—calming the terrors of the
child and
the fears
of the woman, with her
rich,
full,
wrinkled hands.

GRANDMA'S BLUE BAG

A shiny, blue beaded bag in a drawer, hiding beneath cards
and letters.

When we were seven and eight years old, my cousin Donna
and I used to slide the drawer open to find the little bag.

In the bottom of the bag
was a tiny gold pencil—an ancient tool,
a tool that recorded a queue of dance partners in
1927.

I imagined my grandmother as a young girl,

gliding across a dance floor, fumbling with the lace on her
waist, signing up boys to dance.

The bag is still there—tucked in the drawer,
and my grandmother—now ninety-three—

whirls around her golden retriever, seeing only his
shadowy form through her blinded eyes.

And I, now edging towards forty, creep upstairs,
close the bedroom door, slowly open the drawer,
and lift the tiny blue bag with my hand.

I take the gold pencil between my fingers.
I write upon my soul the power of the past,

as the watery, slippery present slithers through my fingers,

like a young lithe dancer slipping from her suitor's grasp.

I Believe

I believe in this moment,
this heartbeat, this breath.

I believe in this space,
this air, this ground.

Yet my mind wanders and
tries to solidify the
intangible—

the future, the past, my
fears.

My mind solidifies the
intangible–

and hangs there,

bewildered–

not knowing

anymore–

what
to
believe.

Unwelcome Bedfellow

The night comes too quickly.

And when I lie down, I am not alone.

Worry squirms beside me, hogging the covers, whining, moaning, kicking, and grinding his teeth.

His flesh is clammy.

His feel, and smell, and sound keep my eyes open—and force me to lose, to lose—to lose—

sleep and peace and calm.

The night comes too quickly.

I rise from my pallet—hoping to leave worry behind—

I look down on him.

I see his deformity, his absurdity,
he is like a dog, chasing his tail.

The night comes too quickly.

I want to open my heart, and abandon the hate.

I want to kick worry out of my bed, wrapping my arms around the quick night, full of love and secrets, full of pause and breath.

Wrapping my arms around the night, murmuring with an anointed language that worry will never, ever understand.

God kept me up last night, my body weary with exhaustion, longing for sleep.

But God kept me up—to whisper secrets to me when She knew all others slumbered.

She whispered—
she longed to show me the
beauty of my soul—
to show me the treasure within—
the treasure that no riches or lack thereof can touch.

I read my soul in the night, by the illumination of Divine sighing.

I wondered at God's wonder, and the inescapability of God's light.

I can be still and know.

God kept me up last night.

I can be still.

I can be still and Know.

Baking Cookies on December 11th

I pushed open the door of the bakery, and leaned outside.

The warm, aromatic air billowed up behind me,
and the freezing awakening air met my face and
arms.

The snow lay all around, barely breathing, hushed,
soothing the city into a chilly sleep.

I stood, feeling the warmth of the bakery, and the stirring
of the cold,

all

at

once.

I stood,
gazing into the face of my Complicated Creator,
cold and shockingly alive,
yet warm and sweetly comforting.

It was one in the morning. I sat in the attic room of a friend's home in a tiny village in Germany. Above my head, there was a square skylight, a skylight that framed a display of gleaming, winking stars. At my feet, a scrawling striped rug of blue, green, yellow, and pink stripes flowed over the center of the wooden floor. I rested on a futon, plump and beige, that presided over the room. It sighed good-naturedly under my weight, and under the weight of blue, pink, and green-furrowed pillows. A glowing lamp burned in the corner like a fading campfire, softly offering its warm embers to the room.

Only thirty minutes before, the room had been filled with my friends, some of whom I had just met. They had told me of their town and their German education. I had spoken of my life in Chicago. They'd laughed as I described my current resolve: "From now on, I'm only going to date guys that own cars, 'cause I'm sick and tired of public transportation!"

Later, one young, thirty-something German was teased that he had a crush on me. His ivory skin blushed pink, and he defended himself. "But I have no car!"

Through the joking and laughter, we'd shared a mysterious familiarity, and my heart was light.

And then, I was left alone, as everyone else headed for bed. I stretched and looked up through the skylight, feeling warm and content. I closed my eyes and listened to the voice of an Israeli singer, David Broza, which emanated from a cassette tape in the silver boom box in the corner of the room. I couldn't understand the Hebrew words, but his song was light and airy, and his exultant guitar held and coaxed me. The warmth in my breast lifted me to my feet.

I began to dance. I danced in the warmth of the lamp, my bare feet gliding across the wooden floor. I sensed the laughter of my friends still hanging rich in the air. I danced with the lightness of the song.

Gratitude began as a diamond in my deepest core and carried me around the bulging futon and across the scrawling rug. With bare feet, I whirled, holding the silk of my skirt about my bare legs. My dance mingled with the remnants of laughter, mingled with wood, mingled with fiery glow, and mingled with reverence for the diamond within. Unexpectedly, I saw myself within a tiny frame of being. I saw myself within a minuscule container of eternity, all of eternity focusing itself in one ordinary, tiny frame of awe.

Broken Heart

As long as my heart is open,
it will surely be slightly broken,
but air and light—imbued with life—
can nimbly caress its jagged curves and crevices.

If my heart is closed,
it may feel protected and safe—
a fortress, a rampart of rage,
but air and light cannot reach in,
and its curves and corners will fill with
stagnation and stink.

Let my heart be open and broken.

As I cry and keen,
let the breezes blow through,

through a space wide enough

for the whole world

to walk through.

Tree/House

When I was little,

there was a tree house up in the field.

It was nestled in the tree line,

the tree line that was destroyed the
day the developers arrived.

It was the boys' place to go,

full of mystery–frightening.

I only saw it from below—
as I gathered a colorful pile of leaves—

my brow furrowed from

worrying,
worrying that I should go home,

worrying that my mother was worrying.

I wonder what sounds rang
through the tree line
the day the bulldozers came . . .

the plywood of the house cracking in half–
cracking with the trees–splitting, shattering, disappearing.

There is another house there now—street
level, carpeted stairs—a family sitting down to
dinner.

I wonder if they ever feel us as they reach for
the salt, or pass the bread—

I wonder if they feel our wildness, our worrying,
our raw, full enjoyment of the trees.

I wonder if they can feel us—or hear our scurrying,

the dry, autumn leaves cracking beneath our feet.

Old Photograph Found—
Warmth, Sighing, and Time

The child has left.

She didn't announce her impending departure.
She retreated silently,
sliding between fragments of memory.

I see her old face now, smooth and innocent,
anxious and plagued with dreams.

I mourn her loss. Her small body, her falls.

I contemplate the body that has grown around
her,
the face that masks her face, the eyes that now
block her gaze.

Where is she now?

Was she devoured whole by the embrace of
warmth, sighing, and time?
Or is she still inside of me–holding up this new flesh, and
coaxing my heart to beat?

Wise Creator, the mystery of aging and change
befuddles and awes me–

One evening, as I enter a crowded room,
I am suddenly struck by the beauty of
a sea of chiseled faces, all graced with graying hair,
and a small inkling of the wisdom of your plan, Creator,
teases my soul.

I struggle to tether this flash of insight,
to place it under my microscope—
to study its intricacies,
so that my own graying hair will not befuddle me so . . .

But the mystery thrashes from my hands and
returns to its ethereal home.

Perhaps, Great Spirit, the goal is not to understand
growing older, to comprehend aging,

but only to fully dwell in the skin I am given,
at whatever juncture I discover myself—
to give thanks for the pimply, adolescent skin,
the twenty-five-year-old glory, and the
dawn of the gray.

Maybe this mystery will be revealed only in small
moments—

moments where—
swimming in middle age,

I look backward and forward—
taking the hand of the skinny little girl with the pixie,
and the hand of the wise old crone with the curious eyes.

The crone, who winks at me through mirrors of years.

Slowly, she draws me forward with her velvety, wrinkled
hand into

a
safe,
veiled space.

TOLERABLE

Holy One,
why should life be merely *tolerable*?
Can't celebration and insight ooze through every moment?
Every interaction?
Every event?

Deep in my core—
I know that this is what I was made for—nothing less.

Enlighten me so that I do not paint myself into a corner of
security and fear.

I want to grasp your hand, Holy One, and leap across the
Michigan Avenue bridge—singing and dancing—throwing
fear into Your back pocket, letting go and letting light
infuse my mind.

Now, Holy One, I am jumping into the river—I am
swimming with the fish.
I am still singing, singing the songs of catfish and trout,

floating, falling, splashing
while Your Voice bubbles in my ears—
gurgling songs of bemusement and comfort.

My clothes are wet.
They stick to my sides—but I emerge from the river,
smiling and happy,
a flapping catfish leaping from my hand.

The Pond

The pond looks like black tar.

Evening is creeping closer, as the sun slips into
her narrow hole behind the trees,

as I imagined she did when I was small.

The pond looks like black tar,

and the sound of shimmering insects hover
above its still water.

If only I could touch the mystery of the pond,

fall into its depths,

to touch and taste the creatures that crawl
beneath her surface.

If only I could,

I might know more of myself,
the parts of me that
appear as tar,
thick, sticky, unrelenting,

but are, in reality,

soft, liquid, and full of
organisms leaping with
untold life.

Life—
that splashes, skims,
plunges, and floats.

Sarasota, Florida—July, 1993. I parked the rental car in the Day's Inn lot, entered the lobby, and used my new, preapproved Discover card to check into the motel.

Later, sitting frozen on the paisley bedspread, staring at the shag carpeting, I mulled over my mission. A month before, I had written to Pat and Ray Donovan of Sarasota, asking their permission to produce a play on their daughter, Jean. Jean, an outspoken, lively, Irish-American woman, had been a missionary in El Salvador during the civil war of the '70s and '80s. At the age of 27, she made a courageous choice to stay in the country, and in 1980, was murdered by the death squads along with three Catholic sisters.

A week after sending the letter, I received a murky message from Mr. Donovan on my answering machine. "We're thrilled. When can we meet with you?" In my letter, wanting to show them the utmost respect, I had requested a personal meeting.

I needed to tell them that I was deeply inspired by Jean's commitment, and that I also knew of sudden, violent death—having lost a brother to suicide—and would approach the project with the greatest sensitivity.

I wanted to tell them of the call I felt to create and produce this play. Only a few months before, I had taken Jean's biography, *Salvador Witness: The Life and Calling of Jean Donovan*, by Ana Carrigan, on a retreat to the Pacific Northwest. As I read her story, I felt a deep call to create a play on the profound commitment she lived in El Salvador. One evening during the retreat, at dusk, I found myself in a darkened sunroom during a thunderstorm. The rhythmic sound of the rain drew me deep into my spirit. As the rain pounded, I could hear one solitary wind chime, dancing back and forth, pulled to and fro by the rain and the wind. This accidental symphony drew me deep within, as I felt the breath of the Divine. That evening, I thought of Jean, and as the wind blew and the solid voice of the chime captivated my spirit, the call to tell her story took root deep within.

And now, months later, the deep peace of that evening seemed a black hole away. I simply stared at the Day's Inn carpeting, wiping sweaty palms on a paisley bedspread, and taking in long, deep, nervous breaths. In, one-two-three; out, one-two-three.

I looked at the clock: 4:55. Ray was picking me up in front of the lobby at five o'clock for our meeting. I took in a breath, exited my room, and walked through the humid, paralyzing air. I stood on the sidewalk outside the lobby, looking for Ray.

An elderly, bent over man shuffled across the pavement. He shuffled past me. A man in his fifties zoomed into the parking lot and jumped out of his car. Too young. I looked right. I looked left.

Suddenly, a tanned, shiny man in a light blue golf shirt slid around the corner. He was about seventy years old. As soon as I saw the Irish twinkle in his eye, I knew. My fear broke in half. He simply said my name, "Lisa," and we spontaneously embraced.

Holy One, thank you for the accidental symphonies that waft into our lives, and draw us deep within, draw us home.

THROUGH

Yesterday at the state prison, sitting in the solarium, the room awash with sunlight, we wrote on the topic, "That day, life loved me." When I gave the topic to the group, Melissa gasped. She quickly began writing. When she read her piece, she reflected on the day that Governor Ryan placed a moratorium on the death penalty and she was taken off of death row. Gail, her skin pale and her brown hair flowing over her shoulders, wrote about the day she gathered enough courage to leave her abusive husband. I penned a short piece about some of the worst days of my life, days that were still "a day that life loved me," simply for the mere reason that I was alive. I was still living, breathing, and moving even through the worst moments. I was puzzled at my own words. "Do I really believe this?" Yes, sometimes. Other days, I rant and shake my fist at the pain. Undoubtedly, I embody both responses to suffering. I move through the pitch dark, often finding meaning in the shadowy realms, but other times, I grope aimlessly, and the impenetrable, secret meanings outwit and outrun me. In the mid-1990s, I sat with a group of German students, and wrestled with these issues, through dialogue and silence.

The sun was sinking outside. The room was growing gradually dark. I sat at a hard, brown table with five German college students and my host, Dr. Detlef Enge. We sat in a cavernous college cafeteria in Trier, Germany. I was touring the country with *Haunted by God*. Detlef had already hosted the play in Trier a year earlier, so, on this visit, he asked me to give a talk instead. Specifically, he asked me to make a presentation on "An American's Perspective of Germany Fifty Years after World War II."

I was nervous. How could I possibly encapsulate into a twenty-minute talk a topic that was so vast and full of pain? I had prepared for the presentation for about a month before arriving in Germany. After I had arrived, I had traveled around the country, performing, and discussing this topic with friends and acquaintances. My friends helped me to explore new insights and perspectives.

In Munich, Robert, a young medical student, standing six feet three inches tall with brown hair and a Bavarian suit jacket, bemoaned the fact that he had learned little about World War II in school. He said that the topic was simply not focused on, especially in regards to the concentration camps. In Bitberg, a fifty-something journalist with ruddy skin, told me that the Jewish people still desire to continue the conversation about the Holocaust—while many others in the country long to drop the subject entirely. I asked him how it could and would be determined that the discussion was over, was complete. He replied, "Well, that is really up to the ones who have suffered the most, isn't it?"

These conversations echoed in my head as I sat in this cafeteria in Trier, my rag-tag crumpled notes before me, and five students politely listening to my words. I spoke of my own German ancestry, and the ninety-two-year-old German woman, Hanni Haase, I had lived with and helped care for in 1993. She had escaped to the United States with her Jewish husband in the 1930s. The students nodded. They seemed moderately interested.

I fumbled with my notes and expressed how I felt that the US had a lot to learn from Germany, especially in regards to the environment. "Your country seems to be a lot more environmentally conscious than ours—especially when it comes to personal lifestyle choices." One of the students rubbed her hands together thoughtfully. Another glanced out the window.

I touched upon the Holocaust, and reflected on my own country, and how my own government has also carried out atrocities beyond imagining—slavery, the relentless funding of war in Central America, and the Vietnam War. The students listened in silence. The sun continued to sink outside. The room grew darker, but no one got up to turn on the lights.

At the end of the talk, I invited questions and comments. One young woman, sitting across from me, with deep brown eyes and dirty blonde hair, spoke first. She exuded a serene intelligence. She said, "I was shocked to hear you say that the United States could learn from Germany. You see, we've always been taught to not take pride in anything German." Another student

chimed in, "Definitely, everyone is so afraid of nationalism." The other students shook their heads in agreement.

A young man with dark brown hair and inquisitive eyes spoke next. "It was hard for me to hear you talk about the shame you feel because of the crimes the US has committed—that really resonated with me—we live with that every day." The blonde woman spoke again, "Slavery wasn't your fault. Why should you feel ashamed? We go to Italy for a vacation—or Amsterdam—and everyone is very nice until they hear our German accents; after that, they become cold and won't even talk to us."

A young woman at the end of the table added, "We weren't even alive during World War II, and yet we're blamed."

I looked at the five students. For a moment, I stared at the top of the table, and remembered my trip to El Salvador in 1994. Most of the individuals in my delegation were Canadian. When one of them was accidentally mistaken for an American citizen, they would vehemently declare, "Oh no, no, I'm not an American!" I recalled the morning when the only other American in the group, a tall pastor from Colorado, had stood up in front at a church service in San Miguel and had apologized to the community. He apologized for the funding the US had given their government, funding that was used to oppress and murder the people. I was grateful for his honesty.

Remembering all of this, I took a long breath in, fumbled with my notes again, and contemplated the faces of the students. No one felt the need to say any more. We sat in silence, the room now almost pitch black. The weight of our governments' terrors bore down on us, and yet our passion to claim our own individual journeys embraced us with warmth and peace. We sat in silence as the last breath of sunlight slipped away.

Finally, the man with the inquisitive eyes smiled and pulled a bottle of red wine from his bag. "I just happened to have this with me."

Someone found seven glasses, and the wine was poured all around. We stood up from the table and raised our glasses.

In the darkness of the cavernous hall, our voices echoed as we sang:

"Shalom, my friend,
Shalom, my friend,
Shalom, shalom.
Till we meet again, Till we meet again.
Shalom, shalom."

Holy One, I am still learning how to move through the painful situations in life. Hold me when the chaos clings to my world, and the impenetrable, secret meanings outwit and outrun me.

But hold me even closer, Holy One, rejoicing with me, when the pieces fall together, and the shadowy realms are infused with light.

Jesus left last night.
He said some words I never imagined Christ would use,
but He shouted them at us and stormed out the door of St.
Catherine's.
He'd asked me to take Him out to get Him drunk, but I'd
refused.
Tears streamed down His face
as He begged me to help Him escape the pain,
"I just don't want to feel anything anymore."
His voice was breaking.

My mind scanned pages from my journal—scrawled with
those exact words "I just don't want to feel anything
anymore."
I gathered these words up and tried to tie them into a rope
that would pull
Jesus out of His despair,
but instead He screamed,
took His name in vain,
and disappeared into the gaping darkness.

I lay in bed last night.
I wondered where Jesus was,
I wondered if He was safe,
I wondered who He was begging from,
I said a prayer for him.
I saw Him on the cross and heard Him breathe,
"My God, my God,
why have you forsaken me?"

Strength for Compassion

Holy One,
the sheer magnitude of suffering overwhelms me, and
often paralyzes me.

Daily I am bombarded with needs—the needs of friends,
family, and strangers.

A woman with uncombed hair in a brown cotton coat
catches my eye on the street. She begs for just enough
change to buy a sandwich.

But my coins are buried deep in my purse, and I am late.
Very late.
I shake my head and continue down the street, as a bony
finger of guilt pulls on my hem.

Creator, embolden me in each new moment so I may be
present and loving to the one who is before me.

But also give me humility.
Help me to hold myself gently when my inner well is
empty, and the strength for
compassion falls from my grasp.

LEVI

I used to call him "Bing."
He didn't look much like Bing Crosby,
but when Levi tilted his baseball cap that certain way,
he reminded me of the old crooner.

When he first came to live with us at St. Catherine's,
Jimmy and I would sing Elton John's "Levon" to him–only
using his name,
"Levi sells cartoon balloons in town."
He would stand in the dining room, listening to us, a bit
puzzled—
but still seeming to enjoy it.

We were trying to break through.

Now, several months have passed, and I'm standing next
to Levi's bed.
I stroke his face, not knowing if he knows I am there. His
arms are pulled up to his chest.
His body is shrunken and thin.
His eyes are only half open, and the outline of his skull
presses against his skin.
I hold his hand.
Tom gently touches his leg.
"Remember when you first came to us, Levi?"
I ask him,
"Remember? We used to sing that song to you?
You probably thought, who are these crazy people? Where
the hell am I?"

My hand strokes Levi's hair.
I bend down low,

still trying to break through.

I sing softly in his ear,
"Levi sells cartoon balloons in town."

I Never Got to Tell You
December, 1991

Dear Venus,

I think of you often. It's still hard for me to believe that you're gone, for you went so quickly. Cook County Hospital failed to contact us after you had died. We didn't even learn of your passing until two months after your death, and there are some things I never got to tell you, so I'm writing you now.

I thank you for gradually, slowly, becoming a friend. You were a mystery to all of us when you first moved in. I remember, one spring afternoon, standing in the St. Catherine's kitchen, my hands plunged into warm, sudsy water. Jimmy opened the refrigerator door, pushed up his glasses, reached into the fridge, and poured himself a glass of milk.

"We have a new guest," he offered, mentioning you for the first time.

I cocked my head in his direction, as I searched with my right hand for a lost sponge.

"But, it's confusing," he confessed. "The name on the intake form is 'Frank,' but I think he might identify more as a woman."

"Pre-op?" I asked, ascertaining that you were in the process of a sex change.

"Exactly."

"Well," I said, "I guess it's up to Frank—we'll call him, or her, whatever he or she likes." "Of course, whether it's he or she, it's up to Frank." Jimmy agreed.

Just then, you entered the kitchen. You came into the room swiftly, but with a distinct air of nobility. You were wearing a blue denim miniskirt, and your caramel skin was shining. Your face was delicate and feminine.

"Hello," Jimmy chirped. "Welcome to St. Catherine's! I'm Jimmy and this is Lisa, and you are?"

You pushed three red plastic bracelets up your arm and snapped your fingers.

"Venus," you announced.

You flashed a smile and flew out of the kitchen as majestically as you had entered.

Jimmy and I looked at each other and together declared, "She!"

Though I was initially impressed by your fervor and pride, as the weeks went by, you seemed to fall into a depression. You put away your miniskirts and bracelets and rarely said a word. You would simply drift through the house, day and night, in that yellow hospital gown—stealing cigarettes. The other guests would complain of your thievery—but you would just silently sit in the corner of the basement TV room, coolly taking drags off a stolen cigarette.

Other evenings I would walk by your room, all the lights would be out, and that white fan would be humming—oscillating back and forth, keeping you cool. I often wondered what you were thinking there in the darkness. I wondered how you were feeling.

The evening our friendship truly caught fire stands out clearly in my mind. I was sitting at the dinner table, stabbing my chicken patty, and groaning about my "tormented life." You sat across from me, quiet as usual, and listened to my tale of woe. I'd had a jaw-clenching, war-ridden day and was feeling sorry for myself. I whined unabashedly to all fifteen St. Catherine's residents sitting at the table. I told them that I'd attended a meeting in the early afternoon, and the tension had filled the conference room as I seemed to conflict on every level with every individual in the room. The strain in the room seemed to violently choke away any real communication or resolution.

Our live-in volunteer, Michael, sat next to me, and in an effort to make me laugh; he stroked his auburn beard and began to recite a list of things I "should've told them." The list included several words I definitely wouldn't have used at that time of my life. After he finished his "suggested tirade," you broke your silence and suddenly bellowed from across the table, "Damn right!"

Everyone laughed. I think I laughed the loudest. A new bond was formed between us.

The next evening, we sat in the basement together on your favorite, knotty couch, which you constantly occupied and rarely shared with anyone else. You told me about your upbringing on the south side of Chicago, and I told you about my childhood in Overland Park, Kansas. You threw your head back and howled when I told you about the Girl Scout den mother who had corralled the entire troupe together at our camp site to chop down a tree and to hurl it down a hillside. The tree had been mutilated by two little Girl Scouts, who had brazenly peeled off the tree's bark with their pocket knives. Our horrified den mother wanted to hide the evidence, for she knew that if the deed were discovered, the entire troupe would be charged for the damage.

"I guess she saw it as a 'teaching moment,'" I quipped.

You laughed and shook your head in disbelief.

A week later, we sat in front of the TV, eating peppermint ice cream. You entertained me by describing your favorite commercials with plenty of expression and bravado.

Next, you showed me your long, red, lacquered nails and said, "Everyone thinks they're fake." I looked at my uneven, unpolished, rugged nails and said, "Yeah, me too." You replied automatically with a long, understanding "mmmm . . . hmmmmmmmm." But alas, you caught sight of my scruffy, unadorned paws and said with a laugh, "Girl, you're crazy!"

Finally, your money came through. The disability assistance you'd applied for was given, and almost overnight you became the wealthiest one in the house. You were finally able to move out on your own. You got a room on the north side, and we all wished you well.

But you kept coming back. I would answer the door, and there you would be, arms full of groceries, saying "Hello" and walking downstairs like you owned the place. Some of the guests even complained that you were once again taking permanent possession of the knotty couch, just like before. I think you were homesick.

The last time I saw you, you were lying on that same couch. I was on my way to the airport. I gently touched your arm and whispered a "goodbye." You looked up at me through half-closed eyes and said, "Lisa, I'm not feeling well." We said our farewells, and I reluctantly left for my trip.

A couple of hours later, your condition grew dramatically worse, so Katia called 911. But when the ambulance arrived, sirens wailing, you refused a stretcher. You stood up, pulled down your black mini skirt, straightened your bracelets, and marched out proudly to meet the paramedics.

Nine weeks later, we learned that you were only in the hospital a few days before you died.

I wish they would've called us.

A month after we learned of your passing, we had a bereavement meeting at St. Catherine's. Tom, Jimmy, and Dave sat across from me. Katia sat to my left. Actually, almost everyone was there, guests and workers.

Your name came up. We talked about how agonizing your loss had been for us, because we had learned of your death so many weeks after your passing. We weren't able to attend your funeral and say our goodbyes, so our grief was difficult to process. But as we shared stories about you, our sadness turned to joy and laughter. We learned more about you by listening to each other. The laughter swirled around the heavy dining room table. This was our memorial service—a eulogy of warm memories and laughter.

The stories were all wonderful, but one in particular stands out in my mind. One afternoon in late spring, two of our guests were walking with you in downtown Chicago. You had just gotten your check, and your arms were heavy with red, turquoise and tortoise shell pumps. You were all chatting away, deeply engaged in conversation, but when one of your friends asked you a question, you didn't reply. Your companions turned to find you, but you were gone.

At last, they caught sight of you several feet back. A Congo band was playing in the street. The drums were banging a rhythm that ached to be danced to, and there you were—dancing—proudly—joyously. You stopped, dropped everything, and began dancing in the street, while the other city dwellers rushed past you, anxious to get somewhere else.

And that's how I think of you now, Venus—dancing—dancing in my memory, and still making me laugh.

Damn right.

With Love, Lisa

YES

For survivors of torture and those who are called to care for them.

She cowers in the corner, gathered up as a fetus in the
womb.

If only she could return to that safety.

Her eyes dart—forth, back,
to the corner, to the floor, to the whirring of the fan.

My eyes glance at her, then away.

My hands touch my waist, my shirt, restless, restless
in the weight of her pain.

Deep in my groin, an expectant God nods to my soul.

"Yes."
"Yes."
"Yes."

I straighten her sheets, I pour the water, with hands as
restless as birds.

I hold her hand during the gyne exam,
while she relives tortures and hands of invasion.

Helpless, my hands push away my hair.
Helpless, my hands wipe away the flow from my eyes.

The relentless God, stirring deep in my groin,

urges,
encompasses,
whispers,

"Yes."
"Yes."
"Yes."

AISHA

Aisha was pregnant two weeks ago.

She sits with our group of nine in the prison chapel.

It's the beginning of our bi-weekly theatre class, and we
are "checking in" to see who is happy, who is sad,
who is peaceful, who is angry.

Aisha was pregnant two weeks ago.

We reach her turn in the circle.
She pulls on her orange shirt, pulls it down over her flat
belly.

Her baby was born.
Aisha left the prison and was taken, her belly bulging, in
handcuffs and ankle shackles to the hospital.

She screamed, sweated, and pushed.

Her baby was born and taken.

Aisha weeps quietly. The rest of us sit.
We sit in barren, shattered silence.

All Is Held

The day before,
my, sister, Shari, had come to my dorm room at Wichita
State University.

It was 7:45 in the morning.

Her presence was odd, strange,
out of the ordinary.

She announced, gently, and with pain, the Unspeakable.

Our older brother,
Mark, dead,

by his own hand.

The fog engulfed us, tears, sobs.

A blue plastic laundry basket,
acting as a suitcase, was wrenched from my closet.

It was filled with underwear, toothbrush, toothpaste,
blue jeans.

Going home.

Immediately.

Now, it is night,
the night of the next day.

I awaken.
Terror pulls me down and pins me to the carpeted floor.

I retreat to the bathroom.

Toilet. Sink.
Tub.

I am shaking.
Every limb trembles.

To-fro,
Head-to-toe.

My body shakes,
images of my brother embedded in each tremor.

Toilet. Sink.
Tub,
all blurs.

I will the shaking to cease, and yet it deepens.

I begin to gasp.

I stumble back to the room.
I stumble back to the bed that I'm sharing with my Aunt
Sharon.

The entire clan has descended on the house.
We are crammed together, sharing beds, sharing blankets.

I crawl beneath the covers. The linens above me shake,
and waves of terror move fiercely through each thread.

My aunt awakens.

She blinks her eyes, and opens her arms.

She holds me under the quaking linen.

She begins to pray out loud.

She smooths my hair. My knee jerks.
She breathes deeply and
invokes the name of God in the darkness.

My elbow rises with a spasm.

"Dear God . . ."

I begin to breathe with her.

My inner eye, clouded and covered, grapples for the face of
the Divine.

"Be with us."

The window above us is open.
A cool breeze exhales through the screen.

I feel the soft sheet, the soft linen
brush against the flesh of my bare, trembling feet.

"Comfort this child."

"Your loved one did not mean to hurt you. Your loved one was in so much pain that they could not see the pain they would cause you."

The words burned on the page. I was holding the latest newsletter of the L.O.S.S. organization of Chicago—Loving Outreach to Survivors of Suicide. In this editorial, Father Charles Ruby was writing directly to survivors.

"Your loved one was in so much pain that they could not see the pain they would cause you."

I had known this truth for years, but suddenly, the words were falling into a much deeper chamber of my spirit. I thought back on my twenties and my thirties, years spent grieving Mark's suicide. I saw the faces of counselors and spiritual directors who had helped me process my grief. I thought back on the last two months of my life. Another romantic relationship had met its demise. This time, the man had proposed marriage, and three weeks after his proposal, had hoarsely whispered his regrets over the phone. I sat on the brown-nubbed couch in the front room of my house, fingering the phone cord, and gasping for breath. "Are you breaking up with me?" I had stammered. "Over the phone? "

I slammed the receiver down, and headed for bed, vowing to stay there for as long as I wished. I thought about this man. I thought of his stuttering words, "I'm just so confused right now."

I realized that I had heard this before. Why are so many of these men confused? Why are most of my friends grounded and centered, and most of my boyfriends seem lost?

A week later, my grief still heavy and present, my concerned friend Karine dragged me to meet with a psychic she had just met. I was skeptical, but I was also out of options. I sat at a small table, and a woman with short brown hair and wire-rimmed glasses looked at me with immense compassion. Instead of speaking of my crushed relationship, as I had expected, she immediately said, "You have an unresolved issue with an older male family member."

"My brother," I breathed.

It suddenly was clear. I was still enraged at Mark. He had left me. He didn't think of me when he took his life. He didn't think of the pain he would create for me, pain that would fester for two decades. He didn't think of my parents or my sister and younger brother. It was suddenly clear. So many of the men I had loved were lost. Mark had been lost. I realized that I had been searching for reconciliation with my brother through all of these relationships. In a matter of seconds, I realized that I didn't want this anymore. I wanted to forgive my brother. I wanted to let go of this pattern.

Two days later, I sat in a quirky restaurant in Chicago's Bucktown neighborhood with my dear friend and mentor, Virginia Smith. We had just begun work on a new play looking at issues of death, dying, and end-of-life care. Virginia knows me well, having directed *Haunted by God*. The sun's rays flowed through the windows. The restaurant was filled with kitschy memorabilia and bright colors. Reds, greens, blues, and bright yellows danced around us. I couldn't hide from her that I was grieving the loss of a relationship and was revisiting my anger at my brother. I spoke of Mark's death and my anger at him that had festered for twenty years. I entertained the remote possibility of forgiveness, and Virginia listened.

She gently touched her plate, knife, and spoon, and began to tell me a story. She said that she had spent many years longing and praying to forgive her mother. Then, one unexpected day, she was out walking her dog, and, as she turned into an alley, a new truth suddenly engulfed her: she had finally forgiven her mother. After years of hoping and praying, the forgiveness slipped through the cracks. It had appeared quietly and unobtrusively.

Her story had settled in the folds of my psyche, and now, a month and a half later, I sat in my office, crying and holding the L.O.S.S. newsletter:

"Your loved one did not mean to hurt you." "Your loved one did not mean to hurt you."

I called a friend. I read the article to her. She listened attentively, as I wept through the words.

I hung up the phone, wiped my eyes and nose with a torn-off piece of toilet paper, placed the article in my backpack, and headed for the train. The sun was shining through the white bulbous clouds above, and a light summer breeze swept over my face. I walked across the bridge that hung over the highway. The speeding cars shot back and forth beneath my feet. Toyotas, Buicks, Saturns, and Volkswagens flashed below me. Banged-up beaters lunged across the concrete, hanging on for life.

I proceeded down Ogden Avenue. The pavement was cracked, and empty potato chip bags and crushed pop bottles lay scattered on the sidewalk. I waited at Milwaukee Avenue for the light to change. The walk signal was illuminated, and I crossed the street and descended into the subway. I paid my $1.75 fare at the turnstile, walked down the stairs, and waited on the platform.

Looking down the tunnel, I saw the light of an approaching train. The rumble of the locomotive filled the cavernous cement station. My hair blew back as forced air plunged through the tunnel. The train stopped, and the doors opened. I stepped through the sliding doors, and as my right foot struck the brown tile floor of the train, a new truth engulfed me: I had forgiven my brother.

Holy One, I am still learning how to move through the painful situations in life. Hold me when the chaos clings to my world and the impenetrable, secret meanings outwit and outrun me. But hold me even closer, Holy One, rejoicing with me, when the pieces fall together, and the shadowy realms are infused with light.

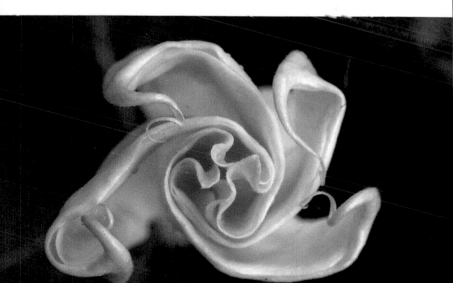

Context and Conversation:

A Dialogue with Lisa Wagner-Carollo

December, 2014

So many people wonder, where are all the spiritual leaders of our time? This is a good question. When we hear stories in the Bible or learn about the lives of saints and heroes of social justice, it seems like their leadership was common knowledge to the people of their day. But what if that assumption isn't accurate? Who are the "Cloud of Witnesses" for our day? I've often thought these folks are just too busy doing the hard work of peacemaking and discipleship to worry about celebrity. So I look around at all the remarkable people in my life and see the goodness of God all around me. There are living witnesses of faith in the midst of everyday life. The regular moments and what we choose to do with them is what makes the difference.

I believe that Lisa Wagner-Carollo is one of these people. She is the founder and director of Still Point Theatre Collective, she has worked in L'Arche Communities and Catholic Worker Communities, and she has led a life in service to the poor and marginalized. She is a dear friend, and she is absolutely committed to living the Christian life in a real way every day.

In order to share the depth of Lisa's contribution to the world, I asked her these questions so that you, the reader, can get to know her better.
—Mary A. DuQuaine, Publisher, Ayasofya Press

Lisa, you have spent a lot of your life serving others in many capacities. What drew you into this kind of work?

My desire to serve comes from my life as a Christian—and I have often found abundant life when I've lost myself in service. The circle comes to mind—Christ calls us to abundant life—and then we answer the call and serve, thus discovering that abundant life. I have also found service to be a path to a deeper understanding of myself and God. I have found, of course, that this discovery isn't all sunshine and praises—I've experienced many sleepless nights along the way. Though I try to commit myself to service, through faith, I still wrestle with my own human life—with insecurities, conflicts, and anger. I love the song "Anthem," by Leonard Cohen. In this piece, he wrote, "To every heart love will come, but like a refugee."

What inspired you to include acting and theater ministry in your work?

My parents both did theater, so I knew from the time I was very young that I wanted to be an actor. When I was five, my dad gutted out an old TV to make a marionette theater for me. I put on shows and also began putting together larger productions with the kids in my neighborhood. We'd perform in the basement or the backyard. As I grew up, I held hopes for a conventional theatrical career. Then when I was fifteen, I went on a church retreat and realized for the first time that God wasn't just someone we spoke of on Sunday mornings—but that God could be my daily companion. I made a commitment to my spiritual life, and found so much joy and strength that I started to think about going into ministry. However, I was still a performer. Finally, after experimenting with this call through a theater company I started at L'Arche and my work with the Call to Action Performing Arts Ministry (creating a play on Dorothy Day), I found a way to fully combine ministry and theater by founding Still Point Theatre Collective in 1993.

What brought you to write this book?

Through the years, I've often relied on writing to process my experiences. This became especially important when my oldest brother, Mark, took his life in 1982. I was eighteen, and he was twenty-three.

I spent a lot of time through my twenties and thirties processing the tragedy of my brother's suicide and allowing the unfolding events of my life to assist in my healing. Writing helped me to crystallize my life experience and healing journey, and became a tool to learn the most from those experiences. I also spent many years reflecting on my encounters with the divine through writing. After two decades of this, I began to gather together the pieces I thought could benefit others—and that is how this book was born.

How did you come up with the title?

It's an expression of my life. A couple of nights ago, I woke up at three in the morning, struggling with a tangle of worries, self-doubt, and confusion. In the darkness, I imagined myself gathering all of them up into a throbbing mass and giving all of this to God. I really felt I had no other choice. That tangle forms the "stuff" of my earthly life as I move above, along, inside and through each experience, but my prayer, my surrendering all of it to the Divine, is also part of my journey. My life with Christ is something I move above, along, inside and through, gathering strength and mysterious insight through the days of my life, even the days when God feels far away.

In the beginning of your book you speak of, "falling in love with the divine spirit." What were your early influences on faith and religion?

My parents were committed to us being involved in church. My grandparents were really deeply involved in St. Luke's Lutheran Church in Kansas City, Kansas. When my grandparents were dating, my grandpa would write letters to my grandma about how concerned he was about the young people in the youth group. It was so cute. They were both very sincere about their faith, and that blows me away. So I think maybe it was genetic! My grandpa would go to church like four times a week. I don't know why he wasn't a minister . . . maybe he didn't have the education to be ordained. My grandpa was a singer as well, so he was at the church singing all the time. And one night—it must have been Advent because it was a Wednesday night service—here's my grandma at home, a young woman with four young kids and she is going nuts with all these kids. My dad was the oldest so she sent him to the church. She said, "You go get your father out of church! He needs to get here and help me!" So he runs to the church and finds his dad sitting in a pew and he tugs on his sleeve and whispers, "Mom wants you to come home." You know, other kids were getting their dads out of bars and my father's getting his father out of . . .

. . . church.

Church! (laughing)

By the time I got to high school, I felt like I just wanted to be a loving person, so I focused on that. I thought being a Christian was about smiling all the time and being loving to people. But that got much harder after my brother took his life. I often tell people that was like switching planets.

After Mark died, it didn't make much sense to live like that anymore. Then I discovered L'Arche and they were talking about how we get in touch with our wounds, and how that's what connects us to each other. Jean [Vanier] talked about letting your woundedness be your doorway to God. God doesn't necessarily take all that away, but instead walks with us through that pain. That made a lot of sense to me.

And I love how Jean used to always talk about people who say, "We're gonna bring Christ. We're bringing Christ." But he would say, "I give you the gift of discovering the Christ that's already there." So that's more my philosophy. I once heard Jean say, "If Christians really believed Matthew 25, can you imagine how different the world would be?" That has really stuck with me. We would be RUSHING to be with people who are broken and suffering, because we want to be with Jesus, you know? We want to be right next to him.

It seems this is all connected to that experience of your brother's death. His life was cut short by his despair. But the impact of his actions has brought this deep transformation that's carried you through your life.

Right. I remember sitting at a retreat—the suicide was not even a year old—and just writing Romans 8:28 over and over again: "All things work together for good for those who love God, for those who are called according to God's purpose." At the time, I didn't really believe it, but I was just trying to make some sense of what had happened and . . . hold on to something, you know?

Do you have words of hope for others who have lost someone?

This is odd but I recently heard something helpful about dealing with loss in the movie "Sleepless in Seattle!"

"Sleepless in Seattle?" Where the mother dies?

Yes, Tom Hanks has lost his wife and people ask him, "Well, what are you gonna do now?" He says, "I'm gonna get up in the morning, I'm gonna go to work, I'm gonna keep breathing, I'm gonna keep going." To be honest, when it's that fresh, I think that's all you can do.

And get a lot of support and counseling. I got counseling right away, because I kept going to the student clinic with some new ailment every week after Mark died. I had a sore throat, then I had chest pains, and when I came in the next week with something new, someone finally had the insight to ask me if anything had just happened. So even though I could barely talk about it, I confided in them and they sent me to the counseling center.

I remember after my brother Dan died, a few days after the funeral, I had an appointment to get my teeth cleaned. I'm sitting in the chair thinking, "Dan's dead and I'm getting my teeth cleaned." It's the most bizarre thing. Because your whole life is shattered and you're wondering how come the world hasn't stopped. Because my world stopped, right?

Yes. It's absurd. It just . . . it just takes time. But healing does happen.

Mark has been gone 33 years now and just a few years ago I reconnected with his childhood friend Lance. They were best friends, inseparable. After graduation, at 18, Lance went right out to LA and started to work in the film industry. Now he owns three vintage movie theaters and in the summer of 2013, I reached out to him and ended up doing a benefit for Still Point Theater at one of his theaters. I'd been afraid to reconnect with him because he had been so close to Mark. Yet now I have this sense of wholeness. Lance and I agreed that Mark's death is part of our DNA, it's part of how we see the world and how we function in it, and that's been a real healing too. Having Lance back in my life is such a gift.

You had a lot to deal with as you moved through your college years. How did that eventually lead you to Chicago?

After I got out of college, I felt drawn to living in a big city. I wanted diversity and I knew I would find that in a large urban environment.

About a year before I moved to Chicago, I had a week off from L'Arche and one of the other assistants in the house, Sister Lucy, told me I could get an inexpensive ticket to Chicago. I was staying with my mom's friend in Rogers Park on the north side of the city, but I was going all over the city by myself. It makes me laugh to think of it because I was so scared; I was sure I would get mugged. I didn't carry a purse or any bags with me because I thought it would make me a target.

This is especially hilarious now because I carry the most bags of anyone I know!

What comes across in some of your writing is the city itself being a kind of character.

Yes, a challenging character! I was so young when I moved here, I was maybe 25 or 26, but I had such a strong sense that I was home. I love the energy of the city and the diversity and the fascinating situations. When you walk out your door in the morning, you never know what's going to happen.

But I also did struggle for awhile. If you don't have a car, you're constantly on public transportation. When I became involved with St. Catherine's Catholic Worker, it was about two hours on public transportation from where I was living to get there. But it was well worth it because I loved being there so much.

St. Catherine's was in Woodlawn, which is on the south side. The neighborhood there was pretty desperate. People were struggling. And that's where I wanted to be. I saw that there had been a lot of suffering in history around race and so I really wanted to be where the pot was boiling around that and try to live my faith there. Either I believed what Jesus said and tried to follow it with all my heart or forget it, you know?

There's people from all over the world here, from all different racial backgrounds, but we have a polarization between parts of the city—north side, south side, west side. But it is an incredibly diverse and fascinating city.

How do you feel the city has influenced you and your work?

When I first got here, I was just meeting so many amazing people who were doing incredible things. Monsignor Jack Egan... Pat and Patty Crowley—the Christian family movement, they started that in the 1940s.

Oh, right.

It was a whole movement to help families focus more on social justice. When I moved to Chicago, I met Patty Crowley. Jack was also still alive when I moved here, and I would seek them out because I thought, as long as they're here and still with us, I want to learn from them.

I worked a part-time job downtown on Michigan Avenue. Patty lived in the John Hancock building and I'd be so tired at the end of the day that I'd just want to go home. But I would tell myself that Patty Crowley will be gone soon and we won't have her anymore. So I'd hop off the bus on my way home and just go up and spend 20 minutes sitting in her apartment with her, absorbing her incredible energy. She was quite elderly at that time, around 90 years old. Sometimes we'd just sing songs, and we'd be talking about something and she'd look me in the eyes and say, "So what are we gonna do about it?"

There was also Dan and Sheila Daley, who started Call to Action. I felt really privileged to work with them for several years. Also, Robert McClory who has written innumerable books. He and I still have breakfast together sometimes. One of my dear friends was Jon Anderson, who was a columnist for the Tribune. He passed away last January. Just having breakfast with him would be so amazing because he had these wonderful stories—he was best friends with Roger Ebert and he used to work for *Life* magazine.

A big part of the experience of Chicago for me is learning from people who are older than me and who have done so much. You meet fascinating people elsewhere, of course, but it's just so much more concentrated here, such a rich environment.

Another thing I noticed in your writing about the city is the experience of traffic.

Chicago traffic! My advice: LEAVE EARLY.

Yeah, leave early, stay calm. (laughing)

And of course, there's the old adage, "There's two seasons in Chicago: one is winter and the other is construction."

But one thing that helps is that we're right on Lake Michigan and that brings me back to calm. I pray and center myself in God by the lake . . . so important. Lately I've been thinking about why we go so fast, you know? What are we racing towards? Because if we really, deeply trust God, why do we need to go so fast?

Sometimes I feel like we're all in a constant state of getting ready for the next thing. Like right now, I'm at the age to start thinking of retirement, and gosh, I gotta get some retirement savings. And even just daily life—some days it feels like it's just task after task after task to get to this goal, to get to that goal, to make that money, to get your paycheck, you know? I get so frustrated because I really don't think that's what we've been created for. But we make it difficult.

We make it harder than it has to be.

Yeah. Years ago, I was at a huge spiritual gathering. Thousands of people. And one morning, we began meditating at dawn, 15,000 silent people sitting around in some big meadow. All the kids in the group are in a children's camp, and at noon, all the children start singing. The silence is broken by these children singing in the distance.

Oh, wow.

And it gets louder and louder, until they get to the meadow and everyone starts to "ohm," until it gets to this intense pitch, and then all 15,000 people whoop with joy. Then they all start drumming and dancing in this meadow! And I was looking around thinking, "THIS is what we were created for!" Not this forced march that we've been doing, you know?

Right!

But then I find myself waking up, checking email, being overwhelmed, thinking, "Oh no, I gotta do this, I gotta get there by this time, I gotta . . . blah blah blah blah!" And all of it has this great intention beneath it, but then it just starts feeling like where's the joy? I believe God wants us to be joyful!

Early in your life you went through several experiences of discernment, of figuring out which way to go in your life. In your book you recall one of those times where you asked yourself, "What have I done? What am I going to do after this?" and you continue . . . "After finally making friends with this unease, I began to let go, and to see my life in sharp relief. One night, I sat and gazed at the stars and realized that without all of the duties that I had let define me, all I had left was the Divine—and myself. I scrawled a poem in my spiral notebook called 'Me, God, and Stars.' Deep in my core, I began to consider the idea that this essential 'beingness' might be enough."

Does your sense of "beingness" help you to continue your work even now?

When I am low and overwhelmed with too many tasks, I try to focus on the fact that all I'm trying to do—and all of my relationships—are an expression of my love for God and God's love for me. I often pray for the grace to see this truth clearly—and to live from that knowledge of mutual love. Beingness has been so important in my growth because I have so many tasks and so many commitments. I feel I've been guided to the practice of beingness to keep myself in balance.

I named our theater Still Point Theatre Collective as a reminder to focus on the "still point" inside of myself where God lives and that cannot be violated. Some days it is easier to access this than others; nevertheless, I try to be gentle with myself in this "back and forth" experience.

I try to make my daily life just like a dialogue with God. I remind myself, "Make sure you pray, Lisa. Remember, deep down, who you really are."

STILL POINT THEATRE COLLECTIVE was founded in 1993 by Lisa Wagner-Carollo, who still acts as the company's Artistic Director. Still Point is a Chicago- based community of artists dedicated to creating performances, workshops, retreats and community events that explore spirituality and raise consciousness on issues of peace and justice. We celebrate the faiths of diverse cultures, inviting all voices to be heard.

For more information on Still Point Theatre Collective, or to inquire about booking a performance, please contact us at:

www.stillpointtheatrecollective.org
Email: stillpointc@aol.com
Telephone: 773-868-1700

PRIMAL ARTIFICE PHOTOGRAPHY, founded by Chris Carollo, is a developing freelance photographic endeavor, working out of the north side of Chicago, focusing on domestic and neighborhood items and icons. The main display focus of Primal Artifice is fine art presentations with occasional forays into event and documentary photography. View images at PrimalArtifice.com